Christmas 2012

To Owen

Enjoy!

Maisy &
PopPop

TRACKING TREASURE

IN SEARCH OF EAST COAST BOUNTY

WILLIAM S. CROOKER

S0-CFC-738

NIMBUS

PUBLISHING

Copyright © William S. Crooker, 1998

All rights reserved. No part of this book may be reproduced, stored in a retrieval system or transmitted in any form or by any means without the prior written permission from the publisher, or, in the case of photocopying or other reprographic copying, permission from CANCOPY (Canadian Copyright Licensing Agency), 6 Adelaide Street East, Suite 900, Toronto, Ontario, M5C 1H6.

Nimbus Publishing Limited
PO Box 9301, Station A
Halifax, NS   B3K 5N5
(902) 455-4286

Cover design: Arthur Carter
Book design: Joan Sinclair

Canadian Cataloguing in Publication Data
Crooker, William S.
Tracking treasure
Includes bibliographical references.
ISBN 1-155109-229-8
1. Treasure-trove — Atlantic Provinces.
2. Atlantic Provinces — History, Local.
3. Legends — Atlantic Provinces.   I. Title
G525.C84 1998   971.5   C98-950015-2

Printed in Canada

Nimbus Publishing acknowledges the financial assistance of the Canada Council and the Department of Canadian Heritage.

In memory of my sister Emily,
whose zest for life was a treasure
to all who knew her.

ACKNOWLEDGEMENTS

First, I sincerely thank my wife Joan for enduring my remoteness while writing this book and for her ingenuity in finding the elusive title.

Second, and alphabetically, a very special thanks to:

Donald J. Bird, Truro, Nova Scotia, who encouraged me to write about the dolmens and provided reams of information on the subject.

Colin Clarke, Waverley, Nova Scotia, who introduced me to the "Mystery Walls" and contributed many Saturdays to studying and surveying enigmatic discoveries.

Bill Mont, Halifax, Nova Scotia, who granted me a generous interview, freely shared his treasure secrets with me and devoted generously of his time.

Frederick G. Nolan, Waverley, Nova Scotia, who most kindly keeps me updated on Oak Island activities and introduced me to his latest discoveries.

Lloyd W. Smith, Sackville, Nova Scotia, who provided me with computerized photographic equipment and spent many hours patiently listening to my long discourses on the book as I wrote it.

And to the following for their kind assistance in contributing some of the grist for this book or referring me to useful sources of information:

Ellis Gertridge, Gaspereau, Kings County
Walter W. Hichens, Crowell, Shelburne County
Wallace Hubley, Seabright, H.R.M.
Glen Johnston, Caribou Island, Pictou County
John Little, East Dover, H.R.M.
William E. Lockhart, Waverley, H.R.M.
Donald Parker, H.R.M.
Orville B. Pulsifer, Halifax
Alva Pye, New Ross, Lunenburg County
Byron Reed, Bedford, H.R.M.

Also, to all those whom I have assuredly overlooked.

CONTENTS

PREFACE • vi

Chapter One   ISLE HAUTE • 1

Chapter Two   THE DOLMENS • 9

Chapter Three   LIVERPOOL BOOTY • 19

Chapter Four   SABLE ISLAND • 32

Chapter Five   MYSTERY WALLS • 47

Chapter Six   THE MONEY PIT • 63

Chapter Seven   NOLAN'S CROSS • 82

Chapter Eight   HENRY SINCLAIR'S CASTLE • 95

Chapter Nine   ANOTHER OAK ISLAND • 114

Chapter Ten   BLONDE ROCK • 122

Chapter Eleven   HALL'S HARBOUR • 129

Chapter Twelve   THE TREASURE WELL OF CARIBOU ISLAND • 134

Chapter Thirteen   JOHN KEATING AND COCOS ISLAND • 146

Chapter Fourteen   GRAVEYARD OF THE GULF • 151

Chapter Fifteen   KIDD'S BOOTY • 157

Chapter Sixteen   ACADIAN GOLD • 170

NOTES • 181

BIBLIOGRAPHY • 182

PREFACE

STORIES ABOUND in Atlantic Canada of loot squirreled away on islands and beaches by pirates and privateers; of fortunes in gold, silver, and precious stones lost in the holds of ships wrecked on the jagged rocks of the rugged coast. Some accounts are documented in historical accounts, while others belong to tradition.

Truly, the east coast of Canada is steeped in the tradition of buried or sunken treasure—almost every harbour, island, or shoal has a tale of long-sought, lost, or undiscovered treasure. Frederick G. Nolan, a renowned treasure hunter, once remarked that the numerous treasure sites on Canada's east coast are no more than one might expect given that the coastline of Nova Scotia alone is more than 1,000 mi. long, about double that of Maine, New Hampshire, and Massachusetts combined, where a multitude of buried and sunken treasures are reputedly hidden.

I became aware of the treasure heritage of Canada's east coast while I was writing my second book on the world's most famous treasure, *Oak Island Gold*. That such an enormous pursuit of treasure was taking place not more than 40 mi. from my home in Halifax, whetted my interest, and I began seeking out other treasure-related tales. *Tracking Treasure* is the result.

Briefly, this book is about lost or undiscovered treasures and the mysteries that surround them. The stories related here are of places where gold, silver, and jewels from various sources and by diverse means reputedly have been lost to the land and sea, the people who may have buried treasure, and those, past and present, who have engaged in the search.

For instance, a typical story covered in this book is of a French war vessel, carrying treasure, that escapes from Louisbourg during the siege. She sails up the Caribou River near Pictou, Nova Scotia, where she is abandoned. Years later, she is discovered beached on a branch of the river, rigging still intact. The loot is missing and thought to be buried somewhere nearby. It has never been found. Another treasure is said to be hidden in a well several miles to the north on Caribou Island. It was deposited by the survivors of a wrecked French pay ship that slipped unnoticed through the British blockade during the Louisbourg siege and foundered on a ledge during a violent storm. My investigations suggest that this legend may be true.

Sable Island, "Graveyard of the Atlantic," has seen more than her share of shipwrecks. Hundreds of vessels were lost to the sands of Sable and many certainly carried treasure. The fragile island sits waiting to release her tragically gotten gains to some environmentally responsible searchers. Much nearer the coast, Blonde Rock attracts so many ships that one wreck piles upon another. Many assuredly hold treasures in their purser's vaults.

In 1307, the king of France attempted to arrest all members of the enormously wealthy order of the Knights Templar. He was successful although a number of knights escaped to Scotland and other countries with their wealth. According to legend, the Templar's fortune was loaded onto eighteen galleys and shipped off to sea—never to be heard of again. According to an historical account, almost a century later Henry Sinclair of Scotland, also a Templar, sails to Nova Scotia, where he builds a castle and other stone structures. Many believe that the purpose of his visit was to conceal a vast treasure. Speculation runs rampant and searches are ever in progress.

Over 250 years ago, pirate Edward Low is said to have buried a treasure on isolated Isle Haute in the Bay of Fundy. In 1952, author Edward Rowe Snow of Massachusetts recovered a small cache of Spanish and Portuguese coins, using a treasure map supposedly drawn by Low. Snow's find is only a tiny portion of the treasure tallied on the treasure map. The main horde has never been discovered.

In 1755, thousands of Acadians were rounded up by the British and deported while their homes were torched and their livestock slaughtered. The Acadians were active traders, exchanging produce from their fertile farm lands for gold and silver. Many are thought to have buried their treasures just before Deportation from which few ever returned. Large caches await discovery.

If, after reading this book, you decide to go digging or diving for treasure, I wish you great success. The odds against finding a single ounce of treasure may be a thousand to one, but the fun is in the search. Even if you never find a single doubloon, you will be well rewarded by the thrill of adventure.

Just a word of caution. You should check with the government(s) having jurisdiction over the area in question to be sure you have the right to dig or dive. You may have to obtain one or more licences and some areas may be off limits for archaeological, conservational, ecological or environmental reasons. Also, make sure you have the right to pass over or "work" a particular property.

If you receive an absolute "no" from the government, don't give up. Laws and regulations continue to be amended, so if you have a genuine interest in a specific treasure or shipwreck, pursue it. Negotiate. If your search proposal threatens a protected site, you may be able to attract the expertise that the authorities will accept— someone who can help you achieve your objective without damaging whatever is protected by law.

Feel free to contact me about any treasure that you are tracking. I'm always interested.

W. S. C.

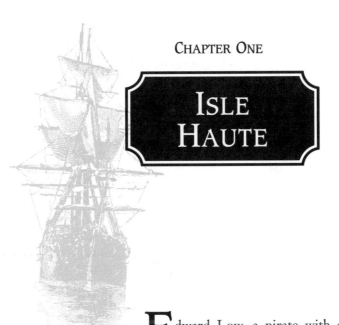

CHAPTER ONE

ISLE HAUTE

Edward Low, a pirate with a passion for cutting off the lips and ears of his captives, reputedly buried a treasure more than two hundred years ago on tiny Isle Haute, 10 mi. out into the Bay of Fundy, off Advocate Harbour, Nova Scotia.

The island was ideal for a pirate to hide booty because of the 40- to 50-ft. tides that limit access to the island to only a few hours each day, and the 300-ft. high rocky cliffs that challenge the visitor to reach the top. Low was caught and hung for piracy before he could retrieve his treasure, but author Edward Rowe Snow, recovered a tiny portion of what may have been the cache in 1952.

Snow, a Massachusetts authority on colonial pirates, armed with a map supposedly drawn by Low, made his way out to the island where he uncovered old bones and gold and silver coins, including a Portuguese gold coin dated 1710. Snow's pirate gold was impounded by Canadian officials, although he was allowed to take the skeletal bones back to the U.S. (after it was established that they were not carriers of hoof and mouth disease).

The pirate map lists the loot in Low's ship, the *Victoria*, as 23,758 pieces of eight and 1,355 pieces of gold.

The French explorer, Samuel de Champlain, discovered Isle Haute during his Acadian voyage of 1604 and named it for its height, *haute* is French for "high." Champlain might have been suitably impressed by this unusual spectacle to give it a less mundane name, but he apparently wasn't given to dramatics.

Back in 1978, when my book about buried treasure, *The Oak Island Quest*, found its way to bookstore shelves, a friend asked, "Have you ever thought of writing a book about the Isle Haute treasure?" I had heard of the island but not the treasure. My interest was aroused as my friend described an awesome island that rose straight up out of the sea and a lost pirate treasure.

"There's a small lake at one end of the island. That's where I think the treasure is buried," he speculated. "Right down there, at the bottom of the lake," he explained, pointing to the floor beneath the dining room table as if it were the surface of the lake. "Someday, I'm going to take my scuba gear over there and have a real good look around."

My friend never did get over to Isle Haute to "look around"—a few years later, he moved to somewhere in central Canada. That was the last I heard about Isle Haute until I recently received a letter from an Andrew J. MacAulay of Alma, New Brunswick, who was looking for information on the treasure of "Captain Edward Low."

MacAulay, a man then in his mid-twenties, wrote that as a fisher of lobster and scallops out of the Alma wharf which adjoins Fundy National Park in New Brunswick, he frequently passes Isle Haute. "As you probably would assume," he wrote, "I travel all around Isle Haute in the fishing season looking for scallops. My curiosity about it grew, so I visited the island for three days with two local school teachers. I didn't know about the mystery of the place, until I saw the mineral claims on the beach." After his camp-out, MacAulay began asking questions. He spoke with Edward Rowe Snow's wife on the phone and learned that Mr. Snow had died ten years earlier. He searched the Halifax Archives and libraries for information, and he wrote to me. He was looking for answers to such questions as . . . had the bones that Edward Snow found been identified, and had anyone else found treasure on the island besides Snow.

MacAulay's letter triggered my memory. My friend's story of 1978 came flooding back: the lake at the end of the island, a treasure hidden in the bottom of the lake. MacAulay had given me a "list" of questions. It would take some time to search out the information he wanted. In fact, it took three years.

My research began with Edward Rowe Snow, the main subject of Andrew MacAulay's letter. Snow first heard of Isle Haute 1n 1945 from Leland Bickford of the Yankee Network News Service. Bickford spoke of the spectacular cliffs that rose straight up out of the sea and of a treasure said to be buried near a large rock.

In 1947, Snow bought a small treasure map supposedly prepared by Low, but it wasn't until 1952 that he definitely identified it as a chart of the island that Bickford had told him about. Once convinced that the map was authentic, he resolved to visit Isle Haute and search for the booty. But he was unprepared for the problems that face the uninitiated visitor to remote Atlantic islands: changeable weather, strong tides, unreliable transportation, and lack of accommodations.

Nova Scotia is almost an island, attached to the mainland of its neighbour province, New Brunswick, by a strip of land only about 15 mi. wide. Because it is almost completely surrounded by the sea, Nova Scotia has a maritime climate of moderate summers and winters, but its weather is dramatically unpredictable. The climate is affected by several conflicting factors: a cold flow of water from the north, known as the "Labrador current," which hugs the Atlantic seaboard on the southern side of the province; prevailing dry westerly winds of continental air; and storms from the south that suck energy and moisture from the Gulf Stream. These influences interact to create unstable weather patterns. Visitors to Isle Haute who choose to stay over for a day or two may find themselves stranded on the island indefinitely due to unforeseen bad weather.

The tides of the Bay of Fundy are among the highest on the planet, ranging from 40 to 50 ft. in height. When the tide rises at Isle Haute, it comes in with a vengeance, rising at an astonishing speed of more than 1 in. per minute. There are two high and two low tides each day, but they occur at different times each day. They advance in time so that each day the tides occur on an average of fifty minutes later than those of the previous day. And they are not consistent in height. As tides are caused by the gravitational pull of the sun and the moon, they vary in height according to the time of month. High tides are higher and low tides are lower at a full or new moon when the moon and sun are in alignment. Tidal ranges are their least when the moon is in the first and last quarter. Consequently, the visitor to Isle Haute must necessarily make arrangements for arriving and departing according to the tides.

Although one could hire a helicopter or float plane, the usual means of reaching Isle Haute is by boat. Several fishermen in Advocate Harbour do provide transportation to the island but, as they are quick to point out, getting there depends on the tides and the weather.

A good time to visit the island is in late spring or early summer when the days are longest and, if you're lucky, when the fishermen

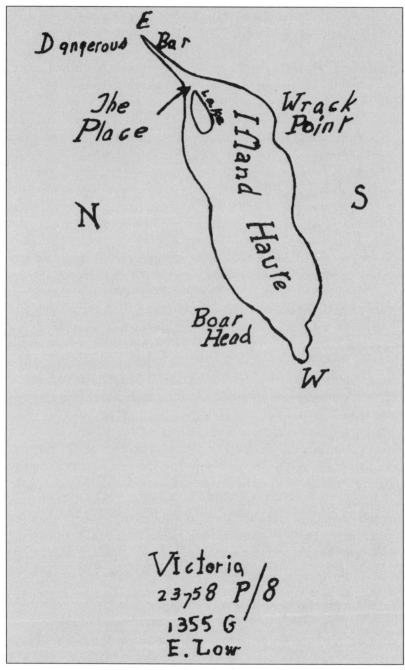

Pirate Edward Low's treasure map indicating the location of his cache at "the place" and the loot of the vessel Victoria *above his name. (Approximate copy)*

aren't busy tending their nets. Choose a day when the tide is high in early morning and plan to leave in the evening. This should give you a half day to explore the island.

Isle Haute is uninhabited, so if you want to stay for any appreciable length of time, prepare to camp out, remembering that you could be out there longer than expected if the forecasted good weather should not pan out.

In 1952, Edward Snow had an advantage over the modern visitor to Isle Haute. At that time the lighthouse on the island was manned by John Fullerton, his wife Margaret, and their fifteen-year-old son Donald. (The light is now automated.) The Fullertons kindly provided Snow accommodations.

Having finalized his travel arrangements, Snow packed his gear, which included a metal detector and picks and shovels, and left Massachusetts for Nova Scotia on June 23, 1952, with his wife Anna-Myrle and their daughter Dorothy. Snow had planned to take his family out to the island with him but was advised on arrival at Advocate Harbour to leave them behind because weather conditions were predicted that could maroon them there indefinitely. Snow found accommodations for his disappointed wife and daughter at a former lighthouse keeper's home and set sail for Isle Haute.

On the trip over, Snow learned from his companions that he was not the first person to search for gold on Isle Haute. Many people had dug there for treasure. In 1925 and again four years later, Dougald Carmichael of Vancouver had searched for Edward Low's loot. It was said that Carmichael had made many friends while digging on the island and had sold stock in his venture. Keeper Fullerton told Snow that there had been two favourite places to search, one in the vicinity of a large rock—probably the one that Bickford of the News Service had mentioned—beside the path that winds up to the top of the island, and the other near the lake at the northeast end of the island. Dougald Carmichael had searched both and even attempted, unsuccessfully, to drain the lake. As to what Carmichael found or didn't find, Snow heard conflicting stories. One was that on his last hunt in 1929 he found both gold and jewels which he took from the island and never returned. Another, by those who claim they were Carmichael's constant companions on the island, is that he never found a coin of treasure in all his searching.

Undistracted by the treasure stories, Snow chose the lake to began his search. His treasure map showed an arrow pointing from the words "the place" to the most easterly end of the lake. Presuming his map to be genuine, that's where he began.

And it was "here" that Snow hit pay dirt. At first, he picked up only pieces of chain or rusted iron with his metal detector as he probed along the northeastern shore of the lake. Then he came upon a pit which presumably had been dug years before by another treasure hunter. It was about 8 ft. long by 3 ft. wide and about $2^{1/2}$ ft. deep. After probing about the pit with his detector, he picked up a strong reaction on the southwest corner wall. He dug a little beyond the southwest corner of the pit and found an iron spike. Tossing the spike aside, he continued to dig and was soon rewarded. First he uncovered the ribs of a human skeleton and then a human skull. By now, night had set in so he postponed further digging until the morning and returned to the lighthouse where he fascinated the Fullertons with his story.

Early the next morning, Snow returned to the pit and uncovered more of the skeletal remains. Moving the soil away from an arm, wrist and fingers, he began picking coins from the soil. In his account of the discovery, Snow, writes: "Again and again my fingers sifted through the dirt seeking and finding the hard metal objects until finally I had quite a collection in my possession. After digging a full 18 in., I tried to get a reaction with my metal detector, but there was no further response." Satisfied with his find, Snow packed up his gear and returned to the mainland. His find consisted of "valuable gold and silver coins of rare Spanish and Portuguese mintages."

But Snow was not allowed to take the treasure back home to Massachusetts with him. Canadian law prohibits people from leaving the country with gold acquire here, so his treasure was confiscated by customs officers and placed with the Bank of Nova Scotia for safe keeping. The coins were later sent to Snow. Experts estimated the 1952 value of the treasure to be about $1,100.

Edward Snow left Isle Haute wondering if Dougald Carmichael had found the bulk of the treasure buried by Edward Low, or if most of it still remained. Maybe the answers to his questions can be conjectured from what is known of the notorious pirate's conduct. Writing about the pirate whose treasure he sought, Snow describes Low as "more fiendish in his captures at sea than any other pirate" and one who "sank to deeds so infamous and depraved that he was finally abandoned in an open boat by his own men."

Low appears to have begun adult life as a decent human being. After going to sea at an early age, Low made his home in Boston during one of visits ashore and earned an honest wage working in a shipyard. In August 1714, he married Eliza Marble of Boston and lived a quiet life at home. But his good behaviour changed dramatically, perhaps triggered by a couple of tragic experiences. His first child died soon after birth and his wife died on the arrival of the second. A short time later, he was fired from the shipyard for quarrelsome conduct.

Not being able to find work elsewhere in Boston, Low again put out to sea, this time as a pirate. From a small boat which he used for stealing logwood and with a crew of only twelve, Low graduated to pirate captain of his own ill-gotten vessel, the *Rebecca*.

As he prowled the seas, leaving plundered and sunken ships in his wake, Low carried out a campaign of terror and brutal deeds. One day, Low and his band of sea marauders, while on a voyage of plunder and pillaging, came upon a very rich prize, the *Nostra Signiora de Victoria*, out of Portugal. As the pirates approached, the captain placed the ship's fortune in a money bag and suspended it out of his window. When Low's bloodthirsty crew boarded his ship, the captain cut the rope and let the entire treasure drop into the sea—better to throw the fortune away than give it to this band of vicious sea dogs.

When Low couldn't find the treasure he knew must be aboard, he tortured some members of the crew into telling him what the captain had done with it. On learning what had happened to the treasure, Low flew into a rage. He had the captain tied to a mast, then drew his cutlass and slashed off the poor man's lips and nose. He then had the cook broil the dismembered flesh and forced the captain's mate to eat it. Then, having worked himself into a wild frenzy by his perverted acts, he had the entire crew of the *Nostra Signiora de Victoria* slaughtered in cold blood.

On another occasion, he had the captain of a whaling sloop stripped naked, unmercifully flogged, and his ears lopped off. He then had the man shot through the head. Two days later, Low indeed went mad. He had the captain of a captured fishing vessel dragged aboard and held while he slashed away at him with his cutlass. Finally, there was little left to maim, he decapitated him in one fell swoop of the cutlass. On the same day, the master of another vessel was hauled aboard. Low cut a hole in the man's chest, pulled out his heart and roasted it on a grill. Repeating the heinous act of the *Nostra Signioria de Victoria*, Low forced the captain's mate to eat the heart. Shortly after, Low had the captain of still another captured vessel hauled on board where he sliced off the poor unfortunate's ears and roasted them over a fire. The roasted flesh was then cut up into small pieces, sprinkled with salt and pepper, and "given" to the captain's crew.

Low's method of torture and murder varied from time to time. Sometimes he simply hung his victims while at other times he was more inventive. It is based on his tastes and flair for gruesome and ghastly acts that I suggest Low may have played a joke on treasure seekers like Edward Snow.

Low's flare for the macabre may have prompted him to play a little trick on future generations. Why else was the "victim" buried with a fistful of gold and silver coins? If he had been apprehended while trying to steal a bit of Low's loot, surely he wouldn't have been buried with his little cache. Wouldn't any sensible pirate retrieve the gold and silver coins before murdering and burying the thief?

I suggest that Low, in a sadistically playful mood, had a grave dug beside the lake for one of his victims—or had the poor bloke dig his own grave—murdered him and placed the coins in the corpse's hand before covering him with soil. Then he prepared several copies of the pirate's map Snow acquired, and made sure they would be around for posterity. Dougald Carmichael acquired one these maps and wasted two trips to Isle Haute in search of what he thought was the treasure of the *Victoria* (probably the Portuguese ship, *Nostra Signiora de Victoria*.)

I don't mean to kick sand in the face of those who would believe that Low buried all the booty listed on the treasure map. But why would he bury a treasure? And, if he did, why would he need to prepare a map to show where he hid it? Surely, his memory wasn't that bad. In his writings, Edward Rowe Snow states that Isle Haute is the only place Low is known to have buried his ill-gotten gains, although his travels took him far and wide. If Low had buried treasure in numerous other locations, as Snow admits may be the case, then a map of the Isle Haute would be reasonable. But, why have no other maps by Low surfaced?

Still, there are those who may be driven to pursue Low's treasure. After all, Low may have had reasons for preparing the map other than those suggested here. Perhaps the map was intended to be handed down to other treasure seekers like himself, after his demise.

The bulk of Low's treasure may, indeed, be waiting on Isle Haute, buried far too deep for metal detectors to locate, waiting for just the right person to come along and unveil a piratical hoard!

CHAPTER TWO

THE
DOLMENS

In 1989, Donald J. Bird, nephew of the renowned author Will R. Bird and a retired civil engineer and amateur archaeologist of Truro, Nova Scotia, reiterated a plea for foresters and others employed in the forests, to be on the lookout for unusual stone formations. His request appeared in an article titled "Ancient Celts in Nova Scotia," published in a newsletter for forest workers in Nova Scotia. Bird's solicitations were prompted by the dawning theory that the east coast of North America was visited by people from Europe or Africa over two thousand years ago, and by a local discovery speculated to be on the site of an ancient settlement that may conceal priceless artifacts and other valuables.

Shortly before making his request in the 1989 article, Bird had visited a site about 3 mi. back in the bush behind the Halifax International Airport, which may indicate the workings of pre-Columbian visitors. There, a thick tabletop-shaped boulder weighing about 25 tons is perched on three stone legs. This megalithic structure, popularly known as a "dolmen," rests on a granite rock platform protruding out of a peat-moss bog. Nearby is another stone about 3 ft. square and standing on four small stone legs.

Another dolmen, with approximately the same typology as the larger, is situated about 15 mi. to the southwest near the famous "Rocking Stone" at Kidston Lake. Still other similar stones are found closer to the airport and on the same general southwest line. One is perched on the edge of a sheer rock cliff overlooking Bedford Basin in Admiral's Park and another in a wilderness area west of Lake Williams, in Waverley.

Donald Bird's quest for local information on odd rock formations took root when he noted that mention of Nova Scotia was largely missing from books he had read that offer evidence of pre-Columbian visitors to North America. A wide range of petroglyphs, stone structures and Norse carvings are suggested as proof that people from Europe had visited North America—particularly the eastern seaboard—long before Columbus, but these artifacts are mostly confined to the Unites States. Bird says, "Except for a slab of rock in the Yarmouth museum called the 'Runic Stone'[1] and an ancient axe from Tor Bay,[2] Nova Scotia is not mentioned. Very few traces of the work of prehistoric people can be found in Eastern Canada. A few sites of Viking settlements are known, but in general, Maritime archaeologists have had to be content with heaps and burial sites of the aboriginal people. Much time has been spent on arrowheads, fish hooks, and animal bone tools. Compared to the wealth of artifacts being found in Greece, Ireland, and Central America, for example, we have practically nothing." Bird was puzzled by this absence of artifacts, especially given Nova Scotia's geographical location relative to the eastern United States.

The southern tip of Nova Scotia is only slightly above the latitude of Boston, and about 100 mi. out to sea from the coast of Maine. The province has a coastline that stretches more than 1,000 mi.—about double that of Maine, New Hampshire, and Massachusetts combined. Significantly, two ways to approach North America were known to early voyagers: the northern route which bypassed Nova Scotia, and the southern route taken by Columbus. Explorers like the Vikings had taken the northern route, so why were indications of pre-Columbian visitors to eastern North America found primarily in the United States? Why would pre-Columbian structures be confined to a small part of the coast rather than being evident to the same extent in Labrador, Newfoundland, New Brunswick, and Nova Scotia?

Assuming that pre-Columbian stone formations similar to those found in the United States are somewhere in Atlantic Canada and conceivable in Nova Scotia, Bird prepared a short article about dolmens and it was published in the June 1988 issue of the "Forest Times." The article endeavoured to inform foresters of the potential for evidence of prehistoric visitors and requested that they "keep on the lookout for unusual rock formations." Bird's article caught the attention of a forest technician, Colin Sibley. He recalled seeing an unusually large rock balanced on a few small stones while surveying in the wilderness area of the Waverley Game Sanctuary, within a few miles of the Halifax International Airport. He returned to the site, took a few photographs and showed them to Bird and others. Enthusiasm rocketed. Was this the kind of evidence Bird had anticipated? Apparently so, since Bird confirmed that, "There was no doubt in our minds that what Colin had found was a table stone, similar to those in New England, which Dr. Fell (Dr. Barry Fell, author of *America BC*) had called dolmens."

Bird quickly organized a party of interested colleges and visited the site by helicopter. His report of the expedition states: "The legs supporting the rock are resting on a small granite dome rising out of the peat moss bog. Around the dome a platform of granite has been laid in a circle. The outer edge is two blocks high and it is about 30 ft. in diameter. On the east of the large rock, on the platform, stands another smaller rock about 2 ft. by 3 ft. and 2 ft. high. It is also supported above the platform by four fist-sized rocks."

The Sibley discovery—dubbed the Sibley Rock—initiated a search by Bird through all the material published over the past century on pre-Columbian visitors. But his conclusions were not what he might have expected. Bird writes:

"In 1984, the National Museums of Canada published a book by Dr. James A. Tuck of Memorial University, Newfoundland, called *Maritime Provinces Prehistory*. There are no structures mentioned in this book, so we could not attribute it [the Sibley Rock] to native people. Looking for people who might have had ships large enough to attempt the Atlantic crossing we discovered that the Phoenicians, before their destruction by the Romans in 160 B.C., had sailed through the Straits of Gibraltar and returned with gold and other metals. The Dept. of Mines and Resources gave us the history of the gold fields of Nova Scotia and the location of all known mining areas. Our megalith was located as near center of all the gold finds as it could be. Had these voyagers 2,500 years ago landed at Cole Harbour and traveled inland by a series of lakes until they reached this height of land? Would further exploration turn up evidence of a smelter and signs of a settlement? Could this larger rock perhaps be adjustable by a few degrees and have been used for sighting the winter solstice and thereby giving the settlement a calendar and a means of knowing their latitude, all important information needed if ships were to be met on the coast. No ancient people left less information behind than the Phoenicians so we very quickly ran out of evidence to support this theory.

"More reading turned up the story of St. Brendan and his crew in their hide-covered coracles. On one of his many voyages he is supposed to have reached our shores. We could not imagine a few monks leaving their boat and traveling 25 mi. inland to erect a 25-ton rock in the middle of a bog. Dr. Fell records many places where Ogam writing has been found in New England but nothing in Nova Scotia.

"Irish mythology was succeeded by the Norse and the story of the Vikings and their voyages to North America has been told and retold over the last one hundred years. There is no record that in Iceland, Greenland, Labrador, or Newfoundland they ever built something like our table rock. Some stone cairns have been found in Labrador, possibly for latitude interpretation, but nothing as massive or of the style we are looking at."

During the course of his research, Bird recalled previously reading a book by Noreen Gray and Annie Smith about the history of the Old Guysborough Road which runs within 3 mi. of the megalith. The book records that a British Regiment had been employed in 1805 to build a road from Preston, a community about 10 mi. southeast of the Sibley Rock, to Goffs, a location on the present Route 212 near the Halifax International Airport, about 5 mi. northeast of the rock. This road had passed very close to the megalith. Bird says, "Suddenly, I felt we had our theory. All the megalith sites we knew about were near former encampments of British Regiments in the period of 1775 to 1812. All these regiments had Masonic Field Lodges."

Bird reasoned that the crew of a Viking ship would not have been able to easily move large stones, but that a regiment of disciplined men could! He says, "I realized that it was a two-hundred-man job and not a twenty-man one." But that wasn't all that decided him against his former Norsemen theories. He says, "One of the greatest puzzles was the smaller stone near the large rock. The one supported above the platform by four fist-sized rocks. Then, one day, I was told that every Masonic Temple must have an altar on the east." So, Bird theorized that the Masons were responsible for the Sibley Rock enigma.

At this point, Bird took his theory to some local Masons who specialize in Masonic history. He says that their "interest was immediate," but he received no official confirmation nor "really" did he expect any. For Bird, it was sufficient that he and his colleges were cordially received and Lodge members looked carefully into his group's suggestions.

Shortly before arriving at his Masonic theory, Bird and his group were introduced to the Kidston Lake dolmen by Janet Kidston who lives nearby. She guided Bird's entourage through the woods to the megalith where they eagerly compared its properties to the Sibley Rock. Bird writes, "It had all the features of the Sibley Stone, a granite platform, and an altar stone, and a lookout rock, which we had also seen at the other site. From my slight knowledge of Masonic ritual I propose to call this the Tyler Rock. The only difference was the fact that the Kidston rock was perched on a natural rather than man-made granite platform."

Letters telling of unusual finds began to come in and Bird makes particular note of one from Wallace MacLean of Merigomish, Nova Scotia, which enclosed pictures of a megalith at Red Bay, Labrador. It was similar in appearance to the Sibley Rock. Bird says that he located Red Bay on a map of Newfoundland and Labrador and wasn't surprised to find the historic site of Fort York only a few miles away and that it had been occupied by the British from 1766 to 1796.

But if the British army did build the megaliths rather than some ancient visitors, for what purpose? Bird suggests that these megaliths may have been used as sites for "Regimental Lodges to hold their meetings, display their regalia and banners, and conduct their degrees, protected from the inquisitive and uninitiated." When a regiment shipped out, it took the knowledge of the meeting place with it. As granite boulders are common features of the glaciated landscape, no one gave a second thought to a boulder resting on three or four small stones. Bird is quick to point out though that this is only speculation and even offers a more practical use for the megaliths: gold mining.

Bird says that before gold mining started in the mid 1800s, the gold-bearing ore was simply picked up off the ground along stream beds. "Hammer mills were not available and if a sledge (sledgehammer) were used the ore would fly in all directions. A large 25-ton rock (like the one near the airport) with a convex base could be rocked back and forth, lumps of ore being pushed under the up side. The large mass moving slowly would reduce it to powder." Bird suggests that after crushing the ore, the rock was leveraged above its bed by

The Kidston Lake dolmen, a large granite pedestal boulder near the famous Rocking Stone at Kidston Lake in Halifax, Nova Scotia. The intervals on the range-pole standing beside the rock measure 12 in.

long wood poles and "mounted on three or four legs while the flecks of gold and the dust was swept up and panned."

Bird suggests that it may be confirmed that all the known dolmens in Nova Scotia are in gold-bearing regions and, furthermore, that the gold ore was bought from the Indians and others who travelled the forests. But because of the value of the metal, "everything was kept confidential including the processing method."

Mega (large) *liths* (stones) are common features in Europe; Stonehenge in England and the large rows of standing stones at Carnac in France are the most famous. The origin, meaning, and use of these man-placed megaliths have been lost in the mists of time. Modern surveying methods, the computer, and epigraphical research have generated much speculation and revealed some facts. Still, archaeologists speak with certainty about these mysteries and the field has been left wide open to those who dabble in the occult. Exception could be taken to some of the odd stone formations like the Sibley Rock and similar ones found in the United States being called dolmens after similar megaliths scattered over Europe.

A "dolmen" is popularly known as a large block of stone supported above the ground by other smaller blocks of stone or by a "stone table." But the most widely accepted technical definition states: "The dolmen is an open sepulchral chamber, usually megalithic, covered by a mound and intended to house several burials."

Therefore, by definition, dolmens are tombs. And, also by definition, what is often referred to as a dolmen is only part of the structure, the mound which covered the megalithic components having eroded away or been removed by human activity. What remains is the skeleton of what once formed the burial tomb. This skeleton which forms only part of a monument is, however, commonly referred to as a dolmen.

Roger Joussaume, in his book *Dolmens for the Dead*, points out that a precise as well as a general definition of a dolmen is not possible as it is a popular term "which has no meaning except in current usage." Joussaume says that, "To the Dane, a dolmen is a closed chamber, outlined by large stones and covered with a slab. To the Frenchman, the word by itself means nothing. And, for the Korean, he considers a dolmen to be a large lump of undressed stone set on the ground above a burial, which may be contained in a pottery urn." There is, however, one component common to all dolmens—they utilize undressed stone. In Nova Scotia, the word "dolmen" is being used in a general way to mean any pedestal boulder whether it may or may not have formed part of a megalithic tomb, the name being derived from the popular image of a "stone table."

I have discussed the Nova Scotia dolmens with several archaeologists and all say that these tabletop stones are natural and not manmade. How did nature make them? One explanation is that after the granite boulder that forms the tabletop portion of the dolmen melted from the glacier at the end of the ice age, it rested on a bed of smaller stones which separated it from a rock outcropping. It takes three objects in tripodal configuration to support an object. The three largest stones in the bed, which were in tripodal configuration, bore the weight of the large boulder above. After a long period of weathering, all the stones smaller than the three largest washed away, creating the dolmen. A less imaginative theory is that the large tabletop boulder came to rest on three smaller stones as it melted from the glacier. But do these theories apply to all dolmens? How can we definitively state that all the dolmens in the glaciated areas of the east coast of North America are accidents of nature?

Donald Bird and his colleagues are convinced that the tier of stones about the circumference of the outcropping supporting the Sibley Rock are man-placed. Archaeologists disagree. But is the glacial erratic theory an easy route out for the archaeologist? Isn't it possible that some of the dolmens are natural while others are manmade? And could some be hoaxes?

On September 27, 1995, the Halifax *Chronicle-Herald/Mail-Star* ran a front page feature titled "On a Rocky Footing." The article begins, "Could a strangely mounted rock near Peggy's Cove hold the key to untold pirate booty? Like many other landmarks of the cove— The Devil's Seat, Halibut Rock, The Whaleback—this rock sits there, huge as life and so obvious. Yet only a few have seen the puzzle and none can solve it."

The mystery rock of Peggy's Cove was discovered by Wallace Hubley of Seabright, Nova Scotia, while hiking the moonscape-like barrens of Peggy's Cove. High on a granite outcrop summit in view of Peggy's Cove and the highway that passes it, Wallace stumbled upon a 150-ton granite boulder perched on three iron cubes about 3 in. high by 3 in. square. The cubes support the megalith in tripodal fashion with two near the sides of one end and the third centred near the other end.

Staff reporter, Tom Peters, author of the article, asks, "Is it [the megalith] a complex map leading to pirate gold? Is it a navigational point set up during the days of sail to warn seafarers of the treacherous Peggy's Cove rocks? Is it a massive granite headstone, solemnly placed to mourn the loss of many lives at sea?" Peters asks the reader to take his or her pick as experts don't seem to have an answer.

Hubley had had scrapings from the iron cubes analyzed at the Technical University of Nova Scotia but other than being able to ascertain that they were 84 per cent iron, the University was unable to determine their age. Inquires of the Nova Scotia Archives and other informed sources had added nothing to his quest for information. No one had any knowledge of the rock.

The day following Tom Peters' article, the Halifax *Chronicle-Herald/Mail-Star* issued another release on the rock titled, "Mystery Solved: Blacksmith Pegged Rock." John Little, a metalworker and blacksmith of East Dover (a community near Peggy's Cove) had appeared out of the blue and admitted to raising the rock. The newspaper reported that Little had accomplished the feat using a 20-ton hydraulic jack and bulldozer blades to position the boulder and slide the iron cubes underneath.

I interviewed Wallace Hubley and John Little separately. Mr. Hubley was extremely helpful in giving directions as to the location of the rock and where I might find John Little. He said that he was somewhat sceptical that Mr. Little could have accomplished the feat all by himself as described by the press. But he said he wasn't calling Mr. Little a liar. "It just seems so incredible," he said.

John Little was turning the red hot end of a metal rod on his

Peggy's Cove "mystery rock." A 150-ton granite boulder perched on three iron cubes. John Little of East Dover, Nova Scotia, claims to have constructed the megalith single-handed, using only a piece of road grader blade and a small hand-portable hydraulic jack.

forge when I approached his shop and lingered in the doorway that Sunday afternoon. A seemingly affable man, probably in his late thirties or early forties, Mr. Little put down his work and welcomed me in. I went straight to the point. "I'm writing a book about treasure, artifacts and so on, and I'm including a chapter on dolmens," I said. "Could you tell me about the one you reported to the press last fall?"

Little explained that he had been teaching a course in metal sculpturing about ten years ago at the Nova Scotia College of Art and Design. "I had this student from California who said to me one day, 'Wouldn't it be neat to mount one of those rocks in Peggy's Cove up on legs,' so we did it, but someone came along afterwards and pushed it over." Mr. Little said the student thought that the raised rock would draw attention to the "moonscape" of Peggy's Cove. The student called the area "nature's sculpture court." Mr. Little said that he and the student hoisted a stone about the size of two woodstoves up onto three iron cubes about 6 in. high. A year later he returned to find that someone had removed the legs. It was then that he decided to set up a rock that nobody was going to be able to tamper with. Little said, "I picked one of the most dominant rocks in the area visible from the highway. I said, 'They won't push this one over, by

God.' It was real hairy when I got one end of this huge boulder up a little but it was just enough to slide the iron cubes into the crack."

Little said that he did the work one cold winter's day all by himself, using an 8 in. wide by 6 ft. long piece of road grader blade and his hydraulic jack. He showed me a short piece off the grader blade that he had used and took me behind the shop and found a sample of one of the iron cubes used to prop up the rock.

To be certain that Wallace Hubley and John Little were talking about the same rock, I asked Little for directions on how to find the rock as I had done of Hubley. Little obligingly drew a very good sketch. It exactly matched Hubley's description.

The press wrote that Little had raised the rock as a tribute to the student who had "long since left the province." I was a little sceptical of that motive and asked Little why he had gone to so much work to mount such a large rock. "I was proving a point," he said. "That dolmens may be man-made?" I asked. "Yes," he replied.

As for the question of whether or not some of the dolmens are man-made while others are natural, the archaeologist will probably tell you that they are all erratics. For my own part, I have trouble accepting a couple of the dolmens I have examined as being glacial erratics. I can't put my finger on exactly what makes me feel that way, but it isn't swayed by wanting them to be man-made. These dolmens have a "built by John Little" appearance.

Although composed of natural uncut stones, they are just "too" perfect for my taste to be accidents of nature. The pedestal stones are just too well arranged. On the other hand, others that I have seen are obviously erratics. I realize that by writing this chapter I may be sacrificing my professionalism in the eyes of my colleagues but truth is more important to me than personal esteem. I choose not to limit the possibility of things, and not to "pooh" the opinions of others, unless I can conclusively prove them wrong.

There is much speculation over what these odd stone formations represent. Although the archaeologists and geologists may be tight-lipped, the amateurs have no problem articulating their theories, which include dolmens pointing to ancient settlements containing a wealth in artifacts and valuables.

Some of the dolmens of Europe contained gold found beside the remains of what were probably important personages. Do our east coast dolmens indicate the possible presence of burial sites? The treasure hunters, at least, are optimistic.

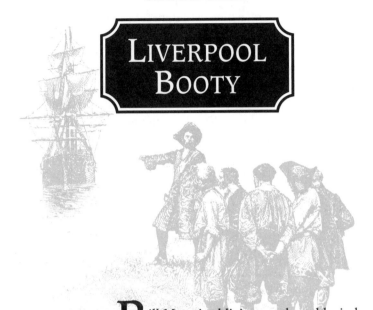

CHAPTER THREE

LIVERPOOL BOOTY

Bill Mont is oblivious to the cold winds and crashing waves as he slowly angles his way between the boulders, trees, and bushes bordering the waters of Liverpool Harbour on the east coast of Nova Scotia. Head bowed, he listens intently for a buzz from his metal detector as he gently rotates it from side to side. Suddenly, a red light flashes on the detector's display accompanied by a sharp beep. Bill lays the apparatus aside and probes the ground with a sharp spade. Then he reaches down and picks something up. "It's only an old piece of rusty wire," he announces and tosses it aside. He doesn't sound or act disappointed. "Treasure hunting isn't for the impatient," he says and continues with his slow and tedious search.

On this October day, Bill Mont, age sixty-eight, Halifax businessman and entrepreneur, is searching for a cache near Fort Point, Liverpool. Although there is lots of work to be done back home, Bill thinks it's time well spent. Armed with maps, drawings, and surveying equipment, I have joined Bill for the day. It's his story I want but the search is enticing. Bill estimates the treasure we are seeking to be worth more than $16 million!

My first knowledge of Bill Mont's treasure hunting activities came in January 1995 when the Halifax *Chronicle-Herald/Mail-Star* ran a story on a dozen or so people who dig or dive each year for treasure in Nova Scotia. The article said that Mont had searched for treasure on Devil's Island at the entrance to Halifax Harbour, and it told of a treasure map which Mont had bought at an auction for $100. The map reputedly gave instructions exactly where and how deep to dig to uncover booty at Fort Point, Liverpool, Nova Scotia. The article also mentioned the treasure hunters of Oak Island, Nova Scotia, which was the subject of two of my past books. So, I filed the article away in my Oak Island scrapbook and there it stayed until I began researching this book. Recalling the newspaper clipping, I dug out the heavy scrapbook and reread the article. Then I called Bill Mont late one Saturday afternoon and set up an interview.

He and I agreed to meet at noon on the following Monday at his office in the former historic Hotel Nova Scotia. I was cordially received by his daughters, Janice and Christine, who help him run his business.

It was as if Bill and I already knew each other; we simply shook hands and got immediately down to business. Bill was known around town as having led an interesting life so I suggested that I might include a brief biography of him in *Tracking Treasure*. Bill unhesitatingly agreed. He also readily agreed to show me the treasure map of Fort Point, but then exclaimed, "Where is the map? I'm not sure what I did with it." "Wouldn't it be in your safety deposit box at the bank?" I inquired.

"No," Bill replied.

"Well, perhaps it's here at your office. Perhaps you tucked it away somewhere ..." Bill cut my prompting short.

"No. It's at my warehouse. Drive me over and we can talk on the way." Bill's warehouse turned out to be more than a half hour's drive away, which gave me time to delve into his interesting life. The printing on the glass window of Bill's office door named three companies: Pleasant Hill Cemetery, Imperial Investments, and Melvin S. Clark. The nature of the first business was obvious, but the second and third were not. Bill explained that Melvin S. Clark was an auction firm and Imperial Investments a flea market business. Did these last two relate in some way to his reputation as a treasure hunter? "I'm a bit of a pack rat," he said, "I always have been. That's how I got into the flea market and auction businesses."

Bill told me a bit about his early days. His father had been a prizefighter who moved from town to town, but Bill never knew him well. He died when Bill was only five years old. "I didn't even know what he looked like until I was about fifty years old and ran across a picture of him," he said. "Then I got tangled up with a step-grandmother who kind of took over from Mother. At one point I landed in the school for bad boys because she wouldn't give me pencils to go to school. She kept saying, 'Get them from the teacher,' but teachers don't really give you pencils. So, I missed school one afternoon and ended up in front of Judge Elliott Hudson. Judge Hudson asked me if I played hooky from school and I said 'yes' so they dumped me in the home."

Bill said that he led his grades in school but was forced into the workplace by age thirteen. The transition from school to a full-time job began with summer jobs. "Each summer while the rest of the kids were playing baseball, I had to work," he said. Bill recalled his early jobs. "My first job was for a woodworking place down in the south end of the city. Then I got a job working in the shipyards as a boiler-chipper and scaler, going down into the bilges and cleaning out the grease: a real dirty job. Then I got on the next summer with the railroad and it ended up that I didn't go back to school. So, there I am, thirteen years old and working on the railroad as a full-time employee. How they dumped me in the hole at nine years old for two and a half years; how they let me out of school at age thirteen is beyond me. It's like something out of Charles Dickens."

The railroad job progressed from "picking up paper on the tracks," to the position of a "redcap" where he "rubbed shoulders" with celebrities. "I still have the tags off the suitcases, like Alan Ladd, Virginia Mayo ... and I carried Ronald Reagan's, the past U. S. president's, baggage. He was a movie actor at that time and I carried his bags up to his suite in that Nova Scotia Hotel."

But Bill had a compulsion to "get away from the cold weather," so he moved to Orange County, California. He had married a girl from Nova Scotia who, he says, "always wanted to come back to her family."

I pulled up in front of the paper-covered windows that hid the contents of Bill's warehouse. Inside lay thousands of cardboard packing boxes containing Bill's auction and flea market merchandise. But where was the map? Bill had recently moved to this warehouse from another. He was sure he wouldn't forget the box he had put it in when he was packing but ... "I think it's this box here," he said and ripped off the tape holding the top flaps together. "No, it's not this one. I think it's that one over there. That large box, with the blue tape."

Two hours later Bill was still slashing open the tops of boxes and I had lost all hope. I sat on one of the wooden sills leafing through a collection of old train photographs. "He's not going to find any treasure map," I thought. But, suddenly, Bill's voice cut the silence. "Found it!" he shouted from the rear of the large room. A moment later Bill stood beside me carefully unfolding a placemat-size sheet of cloth which he laid out on a table. "It's written in blood. I think it has to be blood," he said, running his fingers over the ageing cloth document.

The "treasure map," indeed, appears to be written in blood. No analysis had been made but to Mont and me the lettering and drawings on the document are etched in blood rather than in red ink.

The map is illustrated with the picture of a skull and crossbones, almost identical to the standard warning sign for poison. It is titled "Leeward Islands" and a date is given. Below the title is a description of where the treasure is buried, followed by a tiny grid-shaped diagram beside the four points of the compass; below the grid and compass is a drawing resembling a blockhouse beside a "keep right" warning, and below that a scattering of dots that might represent rocks across which is drawn the Roman numeral "IV" followed by the figures of a fish, a cutlass, and a musket. The document is signed with an "X" and the author's oath, "So help me God."

The written description gives the distance in yards and a bearing of South South-West from a blockhouse. Bill keeps the distance a secret for obvious reasons. The photo shown here was given to me by Bill for publication, and is the same one that accompanied the newspaper article I had clipped several years ago. (The map has been creased to hide the distance.) Since nothing else of significance seems to be concealed, here is the exact text and spelling of the description, as I discern it.

Leeward Isslands, Juli 1811.
The treasure lays in liverpool harber (distance in yards) *S.S.W. frum blok house fort pint*
Ther is 2000 pounds in goold and full 500 pounds silver plat 305 pounds in mexikan dollurs wich the Captin guv ordurs too berry in liverpool harber.
(Beside the drawing of a blockhouse) *Keep Kleer*
(After the Roman numeral, fish, cutlass, and musket)
(X mark) *So help me God*

The map is about 1 ft. wide by 2 ft. long. Mont cut off a small piece of the right top corner of the map and gave it to me for examination and possible dating. I later showed the piece of cloth to a retired chief curator of the Museum of the Atlantic who said it looked like cloth from the backing of old nautical charts. The treasure map had been in an old sea captain's desk when Bill Mont bought it at an auction for $100. It was the property of Annie Ritchie of Liverpool who had lived in a house on Main Street, not far from Fort Point. She sold the house and auctioned off its contents in the early 1990s. Annie, who Mont says is in her nineties, moved to a senior citizens' home in Halifax. The house and the desk that secreted the map had

PHOTO BY THE HALIFAX HERALD LTD.

Bill Mont happily shows off his treasure map from the auction where he purchased it for only $100. Mont says that the map "is written in blood."

belonged to her father. Bill attended the auction and bought the map on the hunch that it might be of value. Bill says that Mrs. Ritchie claims that the map was in the desk as long as she can remember.

When Bill asked Annie Ritchie if "anybody had ever bothered with this," referring to searching for the treasure described on the map, she told him that as far as she knew nobody had. It had always been in the desk.

On the drive back to Bill's office, he talked about his treasure hunting. He first became involved shortly after the end of World War II when he bought a war surplus metal detector. Bill recalls, "It was in a great big olive green suitcase. I paid fifty bucks for it. But it was quite a good instrument and I started searching for treasure with it." Bill read about a lost pirate treasure at Hall's Harbour, Kings County, Nova Scotia, and took a shot at finding it. He says," I went up there playing around a little but I really didn't know where to look." After Hall's Harbour, Bill "went here and there" as he puts it. He searched around the beaches and found a few valuable coins. He probed the sandy floors of a very old house and found coins. "I can't say I found any really big caches," he says, "but I had a lot of fun looking." Bill routinely attended the property tax sales in search of a bargain. And, one day in 1963 he struck it lucky. Two-thirds of Devil's Island near the entrance to Halifax Harbour came on the auction block and Bill picked it up for $600. Bill says that he heard from "one source or another" of a treasure on the island. He searched at the Archives and found out that "some people had been over there a long, long time ago." Bill says, "I never researched it enough, I guess, to really get into it but they claim they were over there digging for treasure."

Bill believes that there is, indeed, a treasure somewhere on the island but he's staying tight-lipped on the matter. As yet he hasn't followed any systematic approach, but he says, "I'm looking pretty hard at having some kind of real serious treasure hunt there." His plan is to lay out a system of lines and conduct a thorough search. "Grid it off and go right from one end to the other," he says.

Before I left Bill's office, we made arrangements to meet at Fort Point to give me an opportunity to get a feel for the hunt. There was always that chance of uncovering a cache and Bill, unprompted, offered me a percentage in exchange for technical help. He said that he would have to give the province and the landowners "a piece of the action," so he would expect to include me in on the cuts.

FORT POINT, near the head of Liverpool Harbour, is a small historical park. Fort Point Lane, a straight stretch of narrow street bordered by immaculately kept lawns and pruned hardwoods, runs out from the end of Main Street to an old lighthouse on the water's edge at the tip of the point. At the back of the lighthouse on higher ground two cannon are mounted on each side of a large stone monument with a plaque commemorating the landing of Samuel de Champlain and others on May 12, 1604, and another plaque giving a brief history.

Scanning the monument's plaques, the word "privateer" caught my eye. The historical write up gives the reputed treasure some weight. It reads: "Licensed by the Lieutenant-Governor, armed vessels owned and fitted out by Liverpool Merchants and manned by Liverpool crews waged war on Great Britain's enemies on the high seas. During the American and French revolutionary wars and the Napoleonic wars, Liverpool privateers protected their own shores and trade and harassed shipping on the American coast, in the Caribbean, and on the Spanish Main. Their prizes, often with rich cargoes, were sold in Nova Scotia under order of the Vice Admiralty Court and enriched the owners and seamen of such active craft as the *Enterprize*, the *Rover*, and the *Liverpool Packet*."

If the treasure map was for real, it was dated in the Leeward Islands in the year 1811. This date fitted the time-frame of the American and French revolutions and the Napoleonic wars. My interest in buried treasure has always been tempered with a dose of scepticism, which tempers my writing. It helps me to rationally examine evidence and to look for logical answers to unexplained anomalies. My scepticism decreased dramatically as I read the inscription. My doubts about the authenticity of the treasure map seemed to be slipping away.

Just then Bill Mont appeared at my side. He had parked his car back near Main Street and walked down along the shoreline to the lighthouse. He was in a characteristically optimistic mood. He had seriously asked me to pack a pick and shovel along with my survey gear when we had talked on the phone earlier in the day, and now his flare for the bright side rubbed off on me. Maybe today would bring one of those unbelievable experiences like winning a $1 million jackpot.

"Well, where do we start?" Bill asked.

"From the blockhouse," I said, although the blockhouse mentioned on the treasure map no longer exists. I was suggesting a lot. Its location would have to be determined.

"But we don't know where it was," Bill said, shrugging his shoulders.

"Isn't it where the lighthouse sits?" I asked, taking liberties with conjecture.

"Why?" Bill asked.

"Because the blockhouse probably had a stone foundation and it wouldn't have been wasted," I said. "The existing lighthouse probably was built on the foundation of the blockhouse."

Bill wasn't convinced. He strolled down from the "privateer's monument" and walked around the lighthouse. "It seems a little low," he remarked. "Why wouldn't the blockhouse have been up on high ground where the cannon and monument are?"

"Why would the lighthouse have been built on lower ground than the blockhouse," I asked. "And, why would the foundation of the blockhouse have been removed?"

Our "whys" were getting us nowhere so we decided to refer to my collection of maps. One was titled "A. F. Church's Map of Queens Co.," dated 1888. It shows a "Fort Street" which appears to be in the same location as the present Fort Point Lane. The street ends in a circle encompassing the words "Old Fort." What appears to be the symbol of a lighthouse is drawn against the northeast edge of the circle, marked by the words "Light Red or Rad." Another undated drawing shows a potato-shaped outline of a road or ditch at the end of "Fort Street" with the name "Old Fort Morris" lettered inside the outline. A lighthouse is shown near the northeast edge of the outline. A note on the drawing reads, "This is a copy of a plan which was drawn by Joseph H. Wentzell from recollection and is therefore not drawn to scale; however, it gives a graphic picture of the general layout of the properties and their owners in 1880 and thereabouts."

None of my drawings showed a blockhouse, so Bill and I decided to seek help—we headed for the nearby Queens County Museum. There, the curator led us to a shelf of old books, one of which contained an old painting of Fort Point. There was no blockhouse to be seen. Furthermore, the painting showed high hills in the background, although the land is relatively flat behind Fort Point. This bothered me, but the curator suggested that the artist had taken "artistic license."

Bill and I were sitting in the museum's reading room discussing our problem with the curator when a gentleman who said he knew some history of the lighthouse appeared out of the blue. "The lighthouse was built on the foundation of the blockhouse," he said, admittedly to my satisfaction. He then gave us details about its construction. The blockhouse was smaller than the lighthouse, but an

The lighthouse at Fort Point. The higher left section of the building is thought to stand on the foundation of the old blockhouse referred to on Bill Mont's treasure map.

extension had been added. If we were to look carefully, he said, we would see that the foundation of the extension is constructed differently than the main part of the building which sits on the original foundation of the blockhouse.

Back at the lighthouse, Bill and I examined the foundation. It was just as the helpful gentleman had said. To me, the foundation of the main part of the structure, which may have been the blockhouse, appeared much older than the extension.

Prepared, at least for that day, to accept the blockhouse and the lighthouse as one and the same, we struck the bearing shown on the "treasure map." We landed in a swamp behind the dwellings on Riverside Drive.

The "treasure map" gives a bearing of South South-West which is $22^{1/2}°$ west of south. But how accurate is this bearing? Pinpointing or recording the location of a treasure cache on land is quite unlike steering a ship on a course towards a point of land. I think a mariner might have taken as much as 10° either side of $22^{1/2}°$ and called it South South-West. Furthermore, magnetic declination is the amount by which the compass needle points to the west of true north, and it varies each year (it varied by about 3´ per year in Halifax

Cove in Liverpool Harbour near Fort Point where Bill Mont thinks that the treasure may have been landed before being buried.

from 1965 to 1975). Records show that in Halifax the compass needle pointed about 13° west of true north in 1750 and had increased to 23°, 195 years later. I had made a stab at what the magnetic declination might have been in Liverpool in 1811.

I would have expected the measurement on the "treasure map" to have been given in rods (one rod is equal to 16½ ft.) as this was the normal land measuring stick of the day. However, it is in yards. One pace for a man of average height, say about 5' 10" is about a yard (shorter men have to stride a bit to make up the difference). Could the distance have been paced off rather than measured? If so, pacing and my more accurate methods of laying out a distance could be at odds.

With the problem of running a magnetic bearing of the year 1811, and not knowing how accurately the distance was laid out, I could only make a few guesses. Besides, Bill didn't like the notion that the treasure was under the swamp so I swung the bearing over onto dry land, giving my guesswork on the magnetic declination a little play.

Bill got out his metal detector and went to work but after an hour of probing, he handed the detector over to me. I was rewarded with a couple of rusty old nails. It was now late in the afternoon and we decided to call it quits for the day.

Bill Mont searching for treasure near Fort Point with his metal detector.

As we packed away our equipment, we mused that it had been a great day. It had been a delightful drive down from Halifax on this beautiful autumn day; we had enjoyed talking to the folks at the museum; we had learned that the lighthouse was probably built on the foundation of the blockhouse; and the surveying and detector work had been fun.

If nothing else ever comes of that day's outing, I learned that treasure hunting is at its best as a sport rather than a greedy drive to become rich overnight. In a way, searching for treasure can be like playing golf with a positive attitude. You might hope to par a hole, but putting the club away after seven strokes isn't bad if you had the fun of trying. And, no doubt, Bill will keep trying to find that jackpot in Liverpool.

FOR THOSE OF YOU who might like to join in the search for Liverpool booty, you could find less promising places to hunt. Bill Mont's treasure map has not been authenticated but even if it should prove to be a hoax—perhaps a practical joke—Liverpool is the home of early Canadian privateers and therefore a likely place of hidden treasure. The wealth of Liverpool was once greatly increased by the disreputable business of privateering. Shipping suffered badly from enemy attacks by armed vessels and the people fought back. They armed their merchant vessels and fitted out privateers to defend their shores. But as well as providing protection, the fleet raided enemy commerce for material gain.

Apparently, Liverpool privateering officially started in 1779 when the citizens who had suffered enormous losses by American privateers petitioned the governor for permission to fit out a vessel and seek reprisal.

Rather than just "a vessel" a number of privateers were fitted out which attacked not only the Americans, but the Spanish and French as well. Among these privateering ships were *Charles Mary Wentworth*, *Duke of Kent*, *Lord Spencer*, *Rover*, and the *Nymph*. All were largely successful and many enemy ships were brought in to Liverpool.

Near the beginning of the American war in the first quarter of the nineteenth century, Liverpool fitted out more privateers, among them were *Liverpool Packet*, *Retaliation*, *Sir John Sherbrooke*, *Shannon*, *Wolverine*, *Rolla*, and a ship owned by sixteen people called the *Saucy Sixteen*.

The *Liverpool Packet* gained considerable fame. She was owned by the Honourable Enos Collins of Halifax, Nova Scotia, commanded by Captain Joseph Barss, and her crew were mainly fishermen. She was captured by the American privateer *Tom*, which was in turn captured and renamed the *Wolverine*. But the *Liverpool Packet* made four particularly profitable cruises before being lost to the enemy. On her first cruise she brought in two ships; the second, one ship and a valuable Spanish prize and about fifteen prizes during the two remaining.

Other successes were the *Retaliation*, owned by Snow Parker, which captured a large number of prizes before being captured on the American coast; the *Shannon*, which made several cruises and brought in a large number of prizes; the *Sir John Sherbrooke*, which brought in several prizes; and the *Saucy Sixteen* which made only one cruise but brought in $1,200 in prizes for each of the sixteen owners.

There is a thin line between privateering and piracy. Is it conceivable that a captain and his crew might not have been indisposed to squirrel away a little more of the loot for themselves than declared to their merchant backers? Is it conceivable that a substantial hoard of treasure lies buried on or near the shores of Liverpool Harbour? Perhaps, someday this question will be answered by a resounding "Yes!"

CHAPTER FOUR

SABLE ISLAND

Situated about 100 mi. off the eastern coast of Nova Scotia, Sable Island lies like a beast waiting for its prey. This 20-mi. long by 1-mi. wide crescent-shaped island, appropriately nicknamed "the Graveyard of the Atlantic," has seen the documented destruction of nearly three hundred vessels and numerous more, estimated in the hundreds, lost to the memory of man.

Being near the main shipping lanes between Europe and North America, and even closer to many colonial routes, Sable Island was a deadly ambush for vessels blown off course or running on an error in calculated latitude. The problem was so bad that by the mid-1700s the island had gained a notorious reputation as the champion wrecker of ships. It had wasted an untold number of vessels and had taken the lives of sailors, soldiers, fishermen, and passengers.

Part of the reason for the violently destructive aspect of Sable Island is the hydrographic nature of the waters that surround it. The island is the protruding portion of a gigantic sand bank on the continental shelf—one of a series of banks that includes the Grand Banks of Newfoundland. Situated at about Latitude 44°N and on Longitude 60°W, the island runs from east to west and is surrounded by shoals stretching for miles. The sand bank from which the island is formed is about 200 mi. long from east to west and 90 mi. wide from north to south. The island is treeless and low, no part being more than 100 ft. above the sea. A sand bar about 22 mi. long stretches out to the west from the western end of the island and a similar bar stretches out to the east from the eastern end. In a storm, a continuous line of breakers stretches over a distance of 50 mi.!

The relative low height of the island makes it almost indistinguishable from the sea on an overcast day and an unfortunate mariner may find himself stranded on a sand bar before realizing that he was approaching the island. Furthermore, mariners say that the colour of the island seems to change to match the water, and storms seem to pounce without warning.

The sand bars are far more dangerous than the island itself. A ship may founder on one of the bars and be washed into a gully, some of which are 30 to 170 fathoms (1 fathom equals 6 ft.) deep, but if a ship runs ashore on the island, there is a good chance of rescue by lifeboat or a line shot out from the shore.

There is some uncertainty about who discovered Sable Island and how it got its name. It is not known if the Vikings reached the island, or if John Cabot sighted it or landed during his voyage of 1497. Some historians believe that the island was discovered by a Portuguese explorer, John Fagundez, in the early 1500s. It has been thought that the island was named after a small furry mammal called a "sable" that was said to inhabit the island, or that it earned its name from shipwreck victims as the word "sables" means "black mourning clothes." However, it is now generally accepted that Sable Island derives from the French name *l'Ile de Sable* (Sandy Island).

NUMEROUS SHIPS carrying valuable cargoes to and from the New World during colonial days met their fates on the sand bars of the "Graveyard," as did Spanish galleons laden with gold, silver, and emeralds following the Gulf Stream homewards.

One of the first documented shipwrecks carrying treasure was that of the *Catherine* in 1737. She was a 110-ton vessel carrying 202 men, women, and children, with a cargo of silver and gold plate and coins conservatively estimated at the time to have a value in excess of £3,000. Among the passengers were wealthy merchants on the way to the New World to establish cloth manufacturing, and individuals and families had brought most of their wealth with them.

The *Catherine* of Workington, Ireland, was on her way from her homeland to Boston when, on the night of Sunday, July 17, she was overtaken by a severe storm and driven onto a sand bar about a mile off the eastern end of Sable Island. The violent wind and current lifted the vessel off the bar and drove it to shore where the raging surf tore it to pieces. All hands were left to the mercy of the waves and pieces of the wreckage. While the surf washed some of the ship's party up on the beach, ninety-eight drowned in the wreck. A few of the survivors died on shore.

In the morning after the catastrophe, the shocked, bruised, and bewildered survivors gathered on the lee side of a nearby sand dune where they chose a spot to build a shelter. There were no trees for lumber, but the storm had cast some of the ship's wreckage up on the beach so they gathered whatever might be useful and lugged it to the dune, where they fashioned a makeshift tent from the ship's mainsail.

For warmth they cut open a number of feather mattresses that had washed ashore and covered themselves with the tick. And they buried the dead.

While many saw to the immediate needs of survival, a few attended to the matter of getting off the island. Their good fortune in washed-up wreckage included a longboat—damaged but not beyond repair. Using tools from a carpenter's chest that had floated ashore, they patched the boat with pieces of boards, staves, and canvas.

Three days after the disaster, the captain, his mate, and seven other seamen set off for Canso, on the east coast of Nova Scotia, about 100 mi. away. They were blessed with good weather and made it to Canso in only two days. Here they were well received by the troop commander of the military garrison and a schooner set sail for Sable Island on Sunday, July 24. It arrived the next day, picked up all the survivors and returned them safely to Canso. News of the saga soon reached New England, and the Boston *Weekly News-Letter* published the story in August, stating that the *Catherine* was accounted the richest vessel that ever sailed from the north of Ireland.

The wreck of the *Catherine* has its special appeal to treasure hunters, for although it is a story of tragedy, human endurance, and heroism, it is also one of "lost treasure"—an indication of the wealth that lies buried in the sands of the "Graveyard."

One of the most popularly known treasure-related shipwrecks of Sable Island is the *Francis*, a 280-ton government transport carrying valuable cargo. It was the last ship to be wrecked on Sable in the eighteenth century. Sailing from England to Halifax, Nova Scotia, in 1799, with forty people aboard, she carried the complete "equipage" of HRH the Duke of Kent (Prince Edward) who later became the father of Queen Victoria.

The *Francis* was making the trans-Atlantic crossing at the peak of December storms because she had been detained in England by an embargo and set sail later than planned. Caught in a hurricane, she was driven towards Sable where she became snarled on a sand shoal miles from land. No one survived to describe the wreck but a good fictionalized version of the disaster is given by J. MacDonald Oxley in his book *The Wreckers of Sable Island*:

> "A few minutes later the *Francis* struck the first bar with a shock that sent everybody who had not something to hold on to tumbling upon the deck—a tremendous billow rushed upon the helpless vessel, sweeping her from stem to stern—their wild cries for help that could not be given them pierced the ears of the others, who would not know but that the next billow would treat them in like manner. Again and again was the ill-starred ship thus swept by the billows, each time fresh victims falling to their fury. Then came a wave of surpassing size, which lifting the *Francis* as though she had been a mere feather, bore her over the bar into the deeper water beyond. Here, after threatening to go over upon beam-ends, she righted once more, and drove on toward the next bar."

Among the victims of the disaster was Dr. Copeland, the surgeon of the Royal Fusiliers on the personal staff of the Duke of Kent, and Dr. Copeland's wife. Copeland was also the Duke's librarian and had supervised the transfer of many valuables from the Duke's English residence to the *Francis*. The Duke had become commander in chief of all British forces in North America in May of 1799 and sailed to Halifax in September. In keeping with his position in the New World, he had arranged to have a magnificent equipage shipped to him. The *Francis* carried his possessions which included silver plate, expensive furniture, books, charts, horses, and all manner of personal effects.

When the *Francis* failed to arrive in Halifax, Governor Sir John Wentworth ordered a search. Sable Island was suspected as the most likely place of disaster. The cutter *Trepassey*, commanded by Lieutenant Joseph Scambler, which was scheduled to sail for Newfoundland, was ordered to stop at Sable Island and determine if the *Francis*, or any other vessel, had recently been wrecked there.

Lieutenant Scambler reached Sable Island on May 13 and went ashore but found no trace of survivors. There was, however, a schooner anchored off the north side of the island that he apprehended and boarded before it could make its getaway. The schooner was the *Dolphin* of Barrington, Nova Scotia, commanded by a Captain Reynolds and laden with fish, seal skins, and seal oil. In his report, Scambler writes, "She had several trunks very much damaged, on board, and appeared to have been washed on shore. One trunk was directed to His Royal Higness Prince Edward, No. 2, another trunk directed to Captain Sterling of the 7th Regiment Foot, both empty. Also a trunk containing two great coats, the livery worn by the servants of His Royal Highness."

Captain Reynolds told Scambler that he had had two men on the island that winter, who were now on board, and when questioned by Scambler confirmed that they had seen the *Francis*, or some large ship, struggling against the currents on about December 22. The vessel tried all day to beat off the northeast bar but without success. At nightfall, the weather thickened and a ferocious storm struck from the southeast. It continued throughout the night and in the morning there was no sign of the vessel; they concluded that she had gone to pieces on the sands. A woman was found on the beach wearing a ring on her finger, and unable to get it off, the men had buried it with her.

Dr. Copeland had been accompanied by his wife and children and their female servant. The only other female aboard was the housekeeper appointed to Lady Wentworth. It was assumed that the body found on the beach was that of Mrs. Copeland as she would have been the only female sufficiently rich to have been wearing a ring of any value.

According to the Barrington Township, Barrington, Nova Scotia, the two men of the *Dolphin* were Coleman Crowell and Ziba Hunt, who had wintered over on Sable Island after having been left there in the spring of 1799 to hunt seals and "look for wrecks." Captain Reynolds tried to pick them up in September but was unable to land due to bad weather and they were stranded there for the winter, surviving on horse meat and berries. When the *Francis* went down, they were blessed with barrels of biscuits that floated in to shore and several cases of liquor. Captain Reynolds returned in the spring, picked up the two sealers and loaded his schooner with some of the booty from the *Francis*. Reynolds didn't report his material gains to the government and "sold and distributed the wreckage stuff all about Barrington." The "stuff" included soldiers' caps, officers' apparel, silk stockings, and red coats. The red coats proved to be the most popular and soon many of the village people were sporting them at public meetings and other gatherings. When the red coats wore out, the women of Barrington wove them into beautiful warm quilts.

But there is another version of the fate of the *Francis*. On June 20, 1791, Louis XIV of France and Marie Antoinette fled Paris with a mob of Corporeal Napoleon's revolutionaries in hot pursuit. Louis had gathered up his most valuable possessions, which included the crown jewels, and with a few court favourites made up a caravan of coaches. His destination was the port of LeHavre from which he intended to set sail for England. Louis and Marie were captured a few days later in Varennes, but the jewels, including Marie Antoinette's 137-carat Regent Diamond, were nowhere to be found. They had been placed in the care of Mary Antoinette's lady-in-waiting who was following behind in another carriage. Although Louis and Marie's carriage was overtaken, the lady-in-waiting escaped. Her driver spotted the ambush from a distance and bypassed it on a side road.

While Louis XIV and Marie Antoinette were apprehended and beheaded, the lady-in-waiting crossed over to London with the jewels sewed into her petticoats. There, she waited patiently for the eldest son of the King of France to successfully assert his right to the throne, as many thought he would, while carefully guarding her secret.

But while the lady waited, she fell in love with and married a Dr. Copeland, surgeon of the 7th Regiment. She revealed her secret to her husband, who in turn passed it on to his commanding officer, the Duke of Kent, who was sent to Halifax in 1799 as commander in chief of the British forces in North America. Dr. and Mrs. Copeland followed in the *Francis* in late December of that year and when the Duke heard the story of its sinking and the salvage by Captain Reynolds, he became suspicious.

Wreckers at Sable Island had long been suspected of robbing and murdering survivors of shipwrecks, so the Duke ordered a Captain Torrens of the 29th Regiment, commander of the *Harriot*, to investigate into the missing *Francis*. The *Harriot* ran into a storm as she approached Sable Island and was wrecked, and only Captain Torrens and a few others survived.

After burying the dead and building a makeshift shelter, Captain Torrens and his dog, Whiskey, set off for the eastern end of the island to check for survivors. There he found a small abandoned hut which he made his headquarters while he scouted the shoreline.

One day when he approached the hut at dusk, Whiskey stopped and began to growl. "What's the matter, boy?" Torrens asked. "Come on now, we're nearly home." The dog crouched down and refused to move.

Leaving Whiskey behind, Torrens opened the door and gasped at what he saw. A beautiful lady sat beside the fireplace drying her long wet hair. She wore the torn fragment of an expensive gown which was splattered with blood, dirt, and sand. Her face was as pale as death.

"Good lord lady, who are you?" Torrens sputtered, staring in bewilderment at the spectacle seated by the fire. "Where did you come from? Are you hurt? You're soaked, You're covered with blood! What happened to you?"

For several minutes the lady stared back at Torrens in silence. Then with her right hand she pointed to the left. Her ring finger was missing and droplets of blood trickled down her wrist. "Murdered!" she said in a hoarse whisper. Glancing around the hut in desperation, she cried, "I want my ring! They took my ring! I've come back to get it."

"Who took your ring?" Torrens asked.

"Those who murdered me for my ring," she replied.

Torrens had some medical supplies in the hut that he had salvaged and reached for them, intending to bandage her mutilated hand. But before he could reach the woman, she slipped by him and vanished out the door. Torrens feared that the woman's trauma had driven her insane and rushed out in pursuit but she was nowhere in sight. "I must be imagining all of this," Torrens thought. "I must be more tired than I realize."

But, when he stepped back into the hut, there was the lady, sitting by the fire. And again she held up her hand to expose the stump of the missing finger. Her eyes pleaded for help. Torrens recalled the story of the doctor's wife who had been found dead on the beach, wearing a ring. He had asked himself the question several times in past months, "Did they really bury her without taking the ring?" It would have been such an easy matter to chop off the finger and remove it, and who would have been the wiser after she had been buried?

"Are you Mrs. Copeland?" he asked. She nodded her head and repeated, "I want my ring. I can't go back without it."

"Go back where?" Torrens asked.

"To rest," the lady moaned. "They murdered me and stole my ring. I cannot rest without it."

Torrens stepped forward to comfort the woman but she screamed, "Don't touch me! Please don't try to touch me. Stand back." Torrens retreated.

"Is there any thing I can do to help?" the captain asked in desperation.

"Yes," replied the lady. "Please find my ring." Then, like a candle snuffed out, she vanished.

A short time later, Torrens and the other survivors were rescued from the island. Back in Halifax, Torrens heard of the wreckers who lived in Barrington. He went there and inquired about the *Francis* and was given the name of Coleman Crowell. After persistent questioning, Crowell told Torrens that a man living in Salmon River, in Yarmouth County, knew where the ring was. When Torrens learned that the man was working in Labrador, he quickly endeared himself to the man's family and was invited to dinner. During the meal, Torrens flashed a gaudy ring that he had bought in Halifax with the intent of using it on just such an occasion.

"Oh, what a gorgeous ring," one of the daughters exclaimed.

"Yes, it is," Torrens replied. "It has been in my family for centuries and bears the family crest. I use it to imprint the wax when I seal letters."

"It's beautiful, for sure," the daughter replied, "but it's not as nice as the one Daddy brought home last ..."

"Now, Emily, don't go saying things like that about the captain's ring," her mother snapped.

"Oh, that doesn't matter," Torrens replied. "Tell me about it."

Before the mother could shut Emily up, she blurted, "Papa said he got it from a rich woman's finger who drowned over on Sable Island."

"No, no," the mother protested. "You're wrong, child, Father got it from a Frenchman from Quebec who owed him money. The Frenchman was engaged to some girl and they broke up and the girl gave back the ring. That's all."

"But, Mommy, Daddy said ..."

"Oh he was just joking with you. Telling you bedtime stories," the Mother purred. "Don't mind Emily," the Mother cooed to Torrens.

"Oh, it doesn't matter," Torrens smoothly replied, "I would just like to have a look at it."

"My husband took it with him when he went to Labrador," the mother explained.

"But, Mummy," the little girl whined, "Daddy said he was going to leave it to be sold in Halifax."

While the mother glared at the child, Torrens dismissed the matter with a wave of his hand. "No, matter," he said, "it's only a ring," and changed the subject.

The following day, Captain Torrens struck out for Halifax, where he made for the most prominent jeweller. Torrens said he was looking for a special anniversary gift for his wife, perhaps a ring. The jeweller, sensing that Captain Torrens was wealthy, laid a stunningly beautiful ring on the counter. "This is priceless," the jeweller said, "but I could let you have it for five guineas."

Torrens carefully examined the ring. "Five guineas is too much," he said. "It's a nice ring but not worth that kind of money."

"Oh, but it is," protested the jeweller. "It's very valuable. It's here more or less on consignment from a fisherman from Salmon River. He acquired it in his travels abroad and should be asking much more for it but he's very poor and needs the money. I have advanced him twenty shillings, and as you can see it's worth much more."

"My good man," Torrens replied, "I must tell you the truth. This ring is stolen and I have the authority under the Duke to recover it. You will hand it over or spend the rest of your life in prison. I will cover the twenty shillings you put out as an act of fairness. And, if the fisherman from Salmon River ever comes by, tell him that if he returns to me the finger he cut it off of, he will be paid in full."

The recovered ring was the Regent Diamond, the 137-carat jewel.

Torrens returned to Sable Island to search for the remainder of the crown jewels, which included another sixty-seven carats, but before he was able to uncover anything he was ordered to command a ship to Madras.

THERE HAVE BEEN so many wrecks on Sable Island that it would take a lengthy book to tell their stories. A few of nineteenth-century import are: *Adelphi, Union, Brothers, Elizabeth, Nassau, Agamemnon, Africaine, Maria, Growler, Marie Anne, Guide, State of Virginia*, and *Amsterdam*. Estimates by those who have studied and lived on Sable Island place the number of wrecks in the magnitude of five hundred. Although the basis of the estimate is unknown, it may well be factual. An observer who was shipwrecked on the island in the late 1800s wrote, "Strong winds, blowing sands, exposed forty wrecks in a row and when the sand was blown back it uncovered forty more."

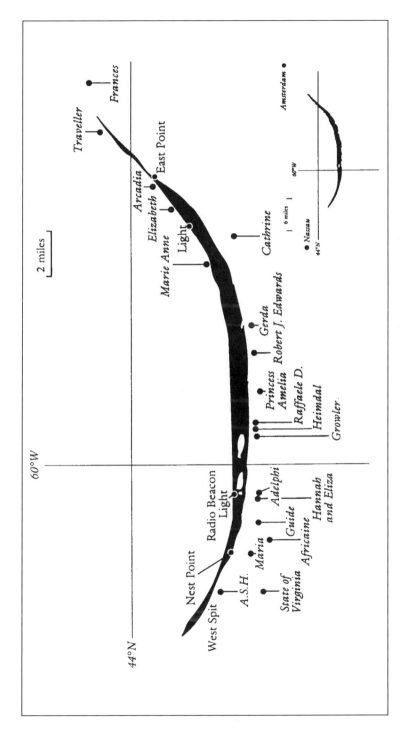

Map of Sable Island shipwrecks by Lyall Campbell showing modern locations of the Catherine and the Francis, *among others.*

Galleons, men-o'-war, schooners, steamers, yachts—ships of all description lay buried in the sands of Sable Island. Who knows what treasure lay in their holds? Chests of gold, silver, emeralds, precious stones, medals, swords, chinaware, muskets—all lost to the sea.

The potential for recovering treasure on Sable Island was expressed by a man who worked on the island, "Every ship or craft of any sort always carried its strongbox, and some of the vessels were well-heeled for trading purposes. All that money is aboard wrecks around the island and it's waiting for lucky finders."

In view of the staggering number of shipwrecks with potentially millions of dollars worth of treasure and artifacts, one might expect the island to be on the top of every treasure hunter's list. However, there are hurdles.

As the western tip of the island is eroded by wave and current, the eastern end builds and moves eastward. A comparison of charts between 1766 and 1767 to 1984 indicates that over this period, about 6 mi. have disappeared from the western end and about 2 mi. have been added to the east. This creates the problem of where to look for a wreck since locations on a chart can only be approximate due to the shifting sands. In his book *Sable Island Shipwrecks*, historian Lyall Campbell writes, "Changes in Sable itself have altered the locations of wrecks vis-à-vis the ends of the island and their bars. A ship that struck opposite the island proper might be shown well out to sea on a modern chart. The *State of Virginia* [a 2,473-ton steamship wrecked off Sable Island in 1879] is a case in point. The *Virginia* went aground well to the east of the west point of the island, but it should be shown well west of it on today's chart."

In addition, there is an environmental awareness and concern for the fragility of Sable Island. It is the unique habitat of numerous species of plants and animals. Strict laws prohibit any activity that might destroy its terrain.

The island's sand is held in place by the intertwining long fibrous roots of the marram grass; the sand dunes would disappear if the grass were destroyed. The island is held together by this grass, under which treasure hunters would need to dig because numerous wrecks now lie buried on the island constantly being recreated by the action of wind, sand, and sea.

According to *Harpers Magazine*, 1866: "There is a prenatural shifting of scenes after every violent storm. Sandy hillocks 50 ft. high that have been landmarks for a generation, have tumbled into the sea; mountains of sand are piled today where yesterday the ground was level as a floor. Old wrecks, long buried, come forth to view. Scores of human skeletons are unearthed. Acres of land have disappeared beneath the sea, and old inlets are filled up, and hidden treasures are revealed."

Following his second visit to Sable Island, Edward Rowe Snow writes in *Unsolved Mysteries of Sea and Shore*, "Winds and sand obliterate everything on Sable Island in time. A full-rigged American clipper ship is encased in one gigantic 90-ft. sand dune; the wind built up the dune until even the rigging and the mast were covered. In spite of shelter fences and other obstructions, the sand sweeps in over buildings, wrecks, graveyards, and everything else man-made. Recent shipwrecks vanish into the sand overnight, while others buried for hundreds of years are suddenly swept clean of their old covering. Only eight craft out of the more than five hundred lost around the island have ever been freed from Sable's sands."

Environmental and ecological concerns have been heightened, and treasure hunting enthusiasm dampened by information about the varying topographic nature of Sable Island. The idea prevails that Sable has been in a long battle with the sea for survival and is losing. Many believe that the island is rapidly shrinking in size—it has been estimated that the island was 80 mi. long at the turn of the fifteenth century and had been eroded down to 40 mi. by the beginning of the nineteenth century—that it is moving in an easterly direction at an alarming pace and that before long it will fall into the abyss that lies off the continental shelf.

Writing in 1963, Edward Rowe Snow stated, "Charts dating back to 1766 show Sable is travelling eastward at the average rate of 1/8 of a mile a year, having moved 22 1/2 mi. farther out to sea from Halifax in 197 years." Snow provides evidence that gives weight to his statement: "At one time, within a twenty-eight-year period, the western end lost 7 mi. The West Light has been moved eastward five times since it was first established, the last move being in 1947. Shoals over which the ocean surges are pointed out as former sites of lighthouses. One of them was so swiftly undermined by the sea that it had to be abandoned within a few hours during a storm. The location where once stood the first superintendent's house is now under 2 fathoms of water!"

But, in *Sable Island Shipwrecks*, Lyall Campbell shows five comparative plots of the island which indicates that the overall movement was only about 4 mi. between 1766 and 1984.

The perception of an island wasting away was initially promoted by the well-intended physician, Dr. S. D. Macdonald, who visited there in 1896. Dr. Macdonald was not only interested in the destruction associated with Sable; he devoted a great deal of time and effort over a period of years to what appeared to him to be the wasting away of the island by the forces of nature, and he published articles on his research. He concluded from records of the Sable Establishment that the island had shrunk by one-half between 1801 and 1886. From this "conclusion" he deduced the size of the island in earlier times. In his "most conservative" judgement in which he allowed for "periods of comparative repose" he concluded that near the end of the sixteenth century, Sable Island was "at least equal to an area of 80 mi. in length, 10 mi. in breadth, and a height not less than 300 ft., with an extensive harbor, having a northern entrance and a safe approach." Looking forward, Macdonald predicted an early demise: "Sable Island," he wrote, "exposed to the full force of the unbroken waves of the Atlantic, before whose power its sand cliffs melt away in a manner that must be seen to be understood, must and will soon disappear beneath the waters."

Lyall Campbell has done much to dispel the notion that the island is shrinking away. In his book *Sable Island, Fatal and Fertile Crescent*, he notes that, "It was assumed that this wasting away was more or less constant, that before the island had been much larger originally, lessening in size with each succeeding century. Modern investigators have proved the error of this thinking. It is likely that the general size and topography of Sable Island have not changed much, that is, 'the volume of land' has remained about the same despite some spectacular short-time changes—since the time of its discovery in the sixteenth century.... The prediction that the island was wasting away has been proved a panicky exaggeration."

Lake Wallace, the main enclosed body of salt water on the island was about 14 mi. long and about 1 mi. wide in the third quarter of the eighteenth century. The lake was open to the ocean and provided a lagoon where ships safely anchored. Later, by the mid-nineteenth century, the lagoon had filled with sand and the lake has diminished in size. Today, Lake Wallace is about a mile in length. In the 1700s, the large lake would have given Sable an appearance of being far larger than the island that exists today even though the land mass remains about the same. As the lake diminished, the island appeared to correspondingly shrink in size.

Sable Island, like any marine land mass, receives its bumps and bruises by abnormally large and frequent storms. Years may pass with

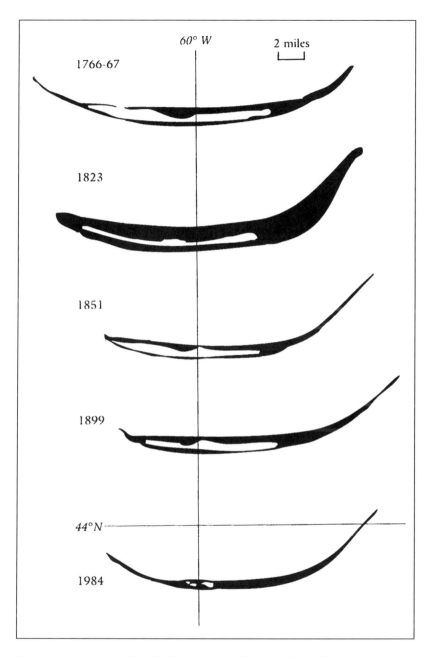

Lateral movements of Sable Island from 1766 to 1984. Illustration from Sable Island Shipwrecks, *by Lyall Campbell.*

no gales greater than average striking and then in one year, several storms might occur to wreak havoc on the shorelines. Living during a time when nature dealt an abnormal number of blows to Sable, its inhabitants and onlookers naturally arrived at exaggerated conclusions.

FROM OUR HOME on a high promontory overlooking Bedford Basin, the back waters of Halifax Harbour, my wife Joan and I often take a fifteen-minute drive to a lookout at the mouth of the harbour to sit on rocks above the pounding surf and watch ships passing up and down the coast. From this vantage point, my thoughts turn to Sable as my eyes scan the horizon in its direction. I envision all the wrecks lying in the sand. I'm not oblivious to the tragedies and loss of life that occurred there, but that's all in the past; the hulks lie waiting to be explored.

Perhaps, in the not too distant future, some ecology-minded treasure hunter, aware of the preservation requirements of Sable will make special and acceptable arrangements with the Canadian Government and mount an expedition to the "Graveyard of the Atlantic." In the meantime, I will continue to sit and gaze across the horizon where Sable lies waiting. It's like looking at an unopened Egyptian pyramid, like waiting to open another King Tut's tomb.

CHAPTER FIVE

MYSTERY WALLS

Fact-collecting of itself is insufficient scientific procedure;
facts exist only as they are related to theories, and
theories are not destroyed by facts—they are replaced by new
theories which better explain the facts. Therefore, criticisms
… which concern facts alone and which fail to offer better
information are of no interest.

JULIAN STEWARD
American anthropologist

A s Donald Bird frequented the Nova
Scotia Archives and scoured library book
shelves for information that might point to pre-Columbian visitors,
Jack MacNab, formerly of Bird's hometown of Truro, trekked the
wilderness lands of Bedford and Waverley, Nova Scotia. MacNab, an
amateur archaeologist and treasure hunter with previous discovery
credits including petroglyphs and shipwrecks, independent of
Donald Bird and his colleagues, was searching for physical signs of a
prehistoric European or North African presence.

In October 1992, MacNab made a discovery which he thought
could rewrite history. Deep in the bush off of Rocky Lake Drive, in
Waverley, he found what he believed to be an ancient dwelling and
possible prehistoric European colony site—a rectangular stone structure without mortar to hold it together. The construction utilized a
vertical wall of bedrock and a natural depression in the ground which
was built up around and enclosed with stone slabs. A large boulder
supported by stones which may have been used for a table was

situated near the entrance of the presumed dwelling. The structure measured about 7 ft. wide by 9 ft. long. It stood about 3 ft. high, but the presence of slabs of rock on the floor suggested that it had been taller at an earlier time. Included in his find were three stone formations which looked like fireplaces. He also reported finding what looked like grave markers. They were flat rocks held in an upright position by other rocks wedged at their bases.

The site was subsequently visited by a professional archaeologist who reported, "It is most likely that the 'structure' was erected as a hunter's blind or possibly as a 'fort' built by youngsters playing in the area. There is no reason to suspect any greater antiquity or more exotic origin of the feature." MacNab's pre-Columbian speculation on the "dwelling" was thus for the most part dismissed and his credibility a bit tarnished. However, the archaeologist's comments fell under scrutiny. In a letter to Dr. David L. Keenlside, Archaeological Survey of Canada, Canadian Museum of Civilization, Bill Lockart, a representative of the Waverley Heritage Museum, commented, "I don't have any big problem with the stone 'house' except I have hunted the area for about thirty-five years and have never seen anybody build something like that. Also, the powder storage huts in the area were built in the early 1800s and were of a different construction. We have found no record of anybody living or working in this area, either Indian or militia or trappers. In our mind it could be extremely old as its location is sheltered and any grouting or caulking would have rotted out leaving the stones in place."

MacNab's stone house was only one of many discoveries. More than four years earlier he had found a petroglyph near Bedford's Lily Lake that had convinced him of the region's prehistorical significance. It was unlike Mi'kmaq petroglyphs. It is an engraving on a large rock of a shield with the Roman numeral IV above it and other symbols that appear to include the sun, moon, a star and a cross. Other inscriptions found on rocks in the Bedford bush lands include what appears to be Egyptian hieroglyphics. Colin Clarke, a professional land surveyor of Waverley and friend of Jack MacNab, sent photographs of the hieroglyphic carvings to the University of Chicago where a professor of Egyptology more or less declared them hoaxes (perhaps because the professor knew for a fact that no prehistoric Egyptian ever set foot on the American east coast). However, it is reputed that MacNab, who has since moved to Vancouver, was so inspired by what he believed were Egyptian inscriptions that he applied for a treasure trove licence (a permit to dig for treasure).

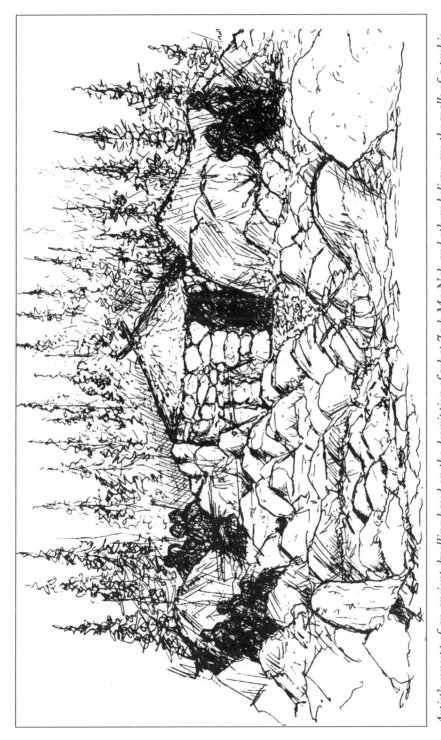

Artist's concept of an ancient dwelling based on the description of what Jack MacNab and others believe are the walls of a prehis-toric dwelling. MacNab discovered the stone structure in the woods off Rocky Lake Drive, Waverley, Nova Scotia.

Jack MacNab seems to have suffered some ups and downs with the scientific community on the authenticity of his discoveries; however, he was involved with one particular find that receives no debunking. It may very well prove to be one of North America's greatest puzzles: the Mystery Walls of Bayers Lake.

In October 1990, MacNab came upon mysterious old rock walls and foundations in the woods near Halifax after being tipped off about their existence by a local aerial surveying firm. "I went to the area they said they were in," he told newspaper reporters. "I couldn't find them and was on my way back when I practically walked into a foundation." Mystified by the find, he immediately escorted Saint Mary's University archaeologist, Dr. Stephen Davis, and Special Places curator, Robert Ogilvie, to the site. Both Davis and Ogilvie were shocked and baffled.

There, on the summit of a rock outcropping, concealed in the thick bush, overlooking the City of Halifax and the Harbour approaches, stands the ruins of what appears to have been an old stone house. Nearby, a massive 3 to 4 ft. high wall complete with gateway meanders over a distance of more than 400 ft., following along the top edges of natural rock cliffs having drops of up to 12 ft. in height.

Davis and Ogilvie were stumped. What was the origin of the structures? What did they represent? Why were they built, by whom, how and when? "It's quite a mystery," Dr. Davis told the press, "It just doesn't make sense; it's not industrial yet it doesn't appear to have been used for long-term domestic stuff. I have no idea what it is." The location of the ruins is being kept quiet pending a more thorough investigation of the site. The ruins are in a location slated for development and the name of the developer is also being withheld.

When queried by the press about the nature of the ruins, Dr. Davis said that the construction style of the walls is Celtic and likely built by people of Scottish or Irish descent. "It's a massive structure, the wall is incredible," Dr. Davis told reporters. "It's very well made. And other curious things are a couple of gates—one of them is directly in front of a steep slope." On January 5, 1991, the *Chronicle-Herald/Mail-Star* reported that Dr. Davis had recently concluded a study "on the historical whodunit." As the mystery had not been solved, Dr. Davis recommended that the site not be disturbed. And, that is the situation as it stands today. For all anyone knows, the site could turn out to be the remains of the oldest European settlement in North America.

While researching for this book, I received a package of aerial photographs, newspaper clippings, letters, and reports from Donald Bird on the subject of the dolmens mentioned in an earlier chapter. While perusing the contents of Don's contribution, I ran across Colin Clarke's name. He had written a letter to Farley Mowat, dated January 18, 1993, asking Farley's opinion on the Mystery Walls of Bayers Lake. The letter was attached to a photocopy of a memo written on correspondence paper of the "Prince Henry Sinclair Society of North America." The photocopy, forwarded to Donald Bird, was a simple note from a person who was sending a photostat of Clarke's letter to another person. Somehow, through the grapevine, a rumour had spread that Clarke had a theory about Henry Sinclair that related to the Mystery Walls.

I immediately called Colin Clarke. Yes, he did have a theory concerning Henry Sinclair and the mysterious walls and he would tell me all about it. And, he would take me to the Mystery Walls. I phoned him on Saturday, and he agreed to meet me the following Wednesday. But first, there was a talk on Henry Sinclair scheduled for the following Tuesday evening at the Maritime Museum of the Atlantic. We would both attend the talk.

The talk, titled "Voyage of the Henry Sinclair," was given by Elizabeth Ross. Her address along with paper handouts told the following story: In January 1996, a ship model—a 45-in. copy of a Viking style in use during the end of the fourteenth century—was unveiled. The ship, scheduled to be built the following year, was named *The Henry St. Clair*. The unveiling marked the beginning of a busy line of events commemorating the 600th anniversary of the voyage from Scotland to North America, led by the Earl of Orkney, Henry St. Clair (also spelled Sinclair).

Although many accepted the idea of Norse visits preceding Christopher Columbus, few knew of the Henry Sinclair expedition. News of the celebration attracted both interest and surprise.

The spark that lit the fire for the organizers of the celebration was a 1961 book by American historian and author, Frederick J. Pohl, titled *Atlantic Crossings Before Columbus*. Pohl established that, aside from the Norsemen, Christopher Columbus was not the first. Henry Sinclair led an expedition to Nova Scotia and the New England coast more than ninety years before Columbus set sail for America.

Pohl arrives at his conclusions through clever historical detective work applied to an account of Sinclair's voyage, published in 1558, known as The Zeno Narratives. Not all historians agree with Pohl but he builds a strong case that Henry Sinclair reached Nova Scotia in 1398, explored parts of the province, lived with the Mi'kmaq and became known to them as the man-god "Glooscap."

The following morning Colin Clarke and I struck out for the Mystery Walls and while we travelled he outlined his speculations. The accepted version of Henry Sinclair's visit to the new world is that he landed at Guysborough Harbour at the head of Chedabucto Bay, on the east coast of Nova Scotia, in the spring of 1398. He sent all his ships back home, keeping only oar-propelled boats; he teamed up with the Mi'kmaq and went about exploring the province; he over-wintered at or near Advocate Harbour in the Bay of Fundy where he built a ship; in the spring he sailed to the New England coast where he did some exploring before returning home.

Clarke believes that Sinclair would not have been so foolish as to send "all" his ships back home and rely on building one on this side of the ocean to return. Furthermore, building a ship to cross the ocean is a big job requiring boatbuilding tools and hardware. Clarke, who once worked in a shipwright shop in Halifax and apprenticed in the ship dockyards for five years, finds the entire scenario preposterous. "He was here to explore, not to build ships," Clarke says. "And, even if he did have the tools with him, where did he plan to find dry wood for the construction?" Clarke isn't saying that it wasn't possible but the story lacks credibility. Clarke suggests that what Sinclair built was a much smaller vessel than a "ship"—probably a 30- or 35-ft. boat. "Something that would hold, say, twenty men. Something that he could go down to Massachusetts in." Clarke suggests that the necessary dry wood may have been hewed or sawed from driftwood logs collected off the Fundy shores.

Clarke says that Sinclair was probably confused about the Atlantic Ocean after crossing over to the Bay of Fundy from the Northumberland Strait. "Here was a great ocean or lake with 50-ft. high tides. It was entirely unlike the ocean he was familiar with. Sinclair must have thought that he had found a new body of water and built a larger boat than their rowing boats to explore it." But, what about the return trip home? Where were the ships that Sinclair was to return home in?

Clarke says that the Indians knew the route from Advocate Harbour in the Bay of Fundy to Halifax Harbour extremely well. They constantly portaged back and forth using the system of waterways which incorporates the Shubenacadie River. The Mi'kmaq probably escorted Sinclair over this route and it would have been logical for him to choose Bedford Basin of Halifax Harbour or the Northwest Arm as a location to anchor his ships for the trip home while he explored the great lake or ocean with the high tides. Sinclair would have left men behind—say forty or fifty—to guard the ships while he was gone.

If his supposition is correct, Clarke says that the men left behind to look after the ships probably moved a bit inland for the winter where there was shelter and game to hunt. They found a promontory where they could live, watch the ships, and keep a lookout for Sinclair's return. They built shelters and, not knowing how long Sinclair would be away, went about the business of building a fort. This work may have been done simply to keep the men busy. But whatever the motive, it was never completed. Sinclair returned at the point at which the construction now exists. "This is all speculation on my part," Colin says. "I could be wrong. Who knows?"

At this point in his narrative, we were on the Bicentennial Highway heading for Halifax. I parked at Colin's request where we could see all of Halifax Harbour as far out as MacNab's Island. "You'll see what I'm driving at in a moment," he said. "The place I'm going to show you is about this elevation and not far away."

Fifteen minutes later we were hiking up a path through the woods. "Man-made trails become animal paths," Colin said, meaning that this was probably the route that Sinclair's men used six centuries ago. Further back, Colin had pointed out ledges of fragmented rock—stone slabs that could be easily plucked and used to build stone walls. In one location, he pointed out a cliff that obviously had been picked bare at an earlier time. Moss and lichen covered the remains of what had once been a ledge of fragmented rock.

Suddenly, we were there! The path popped into a clearing on top of a high outcropping of rock and there stood the stone house. I was stunned. I had expected nothing like what stood before me. Like Dr. Stephen Davis and Robert Ogilvie, I was both shocked and baffled.

The stone "house" is approximately 38 ft. in length, running in a north-south direction. The width of the structure varies from about 23 ft. on the south to about 27½ ft. on the north end. It has a 3 ft. wide entrance on the south end. A pit, possibly the fireplace, 4 ft. wide by 6 ft. long is built against the east wall of the structure near the north end. The walls of the pit are 4 ft. high. The walls of the "house" stand to a maximum height of 4 ft. but many portions may have been equally high or higher at an earlier time as the area within and outside the structure is littered with stones from the walls that

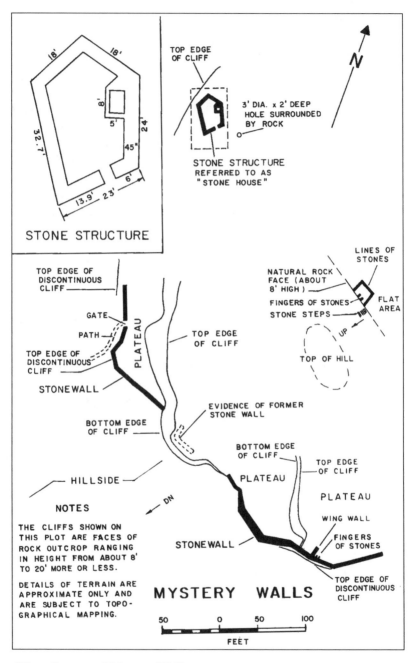

STONE STRUCTURE

TOP EDGE OF CLIFF

3' DIA. x 2' DEEP HOLE SURROUNDED BY ROCK

STONE STRUCTURE REFERRED TO AS "STONE HOUSE"

LINES OF STONES

NATURAL ROCK FACE (ABOUT 8' HIGH)

FINGERS OF STONES

STONE STEPS

FLAT AREA

UP

TOP OF HILL

TOP EDGE OF DISCONTINUOUS CLIFF

GATE

PATH

TOP EDGE OF DISCONTINUOUS CLIFF

STONEWALL

PLATEAU

TOP EDGE OF CLIFF

EVIDENCE OF FORMER STONE WALL

BOTTOM EDGE OF CLIFF

BOTTOM EDGE OF CLIFF

TOP EDGE OF CLIFF

PLATEAU

HILLSIDE

PLATEAU

DN

WING WALL

FINGERS OF STONES

STONEWALL

NOTES

THE CLIFFS SHOWN ON THIS PLOT ARE FACES OF ROCK OUTCROP RANGING IN HEIGHT FROM ABOUT 8' TO 20' MORE OR LESS.

DETAILS OF TERRAIN ARE APPROXIMATE ONLY AND ARE SUBJECT TO TOPO- GRAPHICAL MAPPING.

TOP EDGE OF DISCONTINUOUS CLIFF

MYSTERY WALLS

50   0   50   100

FEET

Plan of survey of Mystery Walls.

have been torn away by nature and human activity. The walls of the structure which are about 45 in. thick are well built of flat stone slabs, carefully placed and fitted and rubble filled. The winding rock walls, about 170 ft. to the south of the stone "house," are equally well built. Carefully placed and fitted flat slabs of stone form the exterior walls supporting rubble stone fill. The walls stand to a maximum of 4 ft. as they do in the stone house and have also undergone a fair amount of destruction, thus decreasing their original heights in various places. The thickness of the walls is generally about 3 ft. but reaches a width of about 7 ft. in one section where soil appears to have been incorporated in the construction.

The entrance to the stone house at Mystery Walls. Each interval on the range pole equals 12 in.

About 200 ft. southwest of the stone house is what appears to be the foundation of another dwelling. It was discovered by Colin Clarke during a visit to the ruins with Jack MacNab. Three lines of stones, beneath and protruding through the moss of the forest floor, are incorporated with a vertical section of bedrock to form a rectangular structure approximately 20 ft. southeast by 17 ft. southwest. A stairway of hand-placed flat stone slabs, partly covered by moss, begins at the outside southern corner of the "foundation" at the base of the face of the bedrock and climbs toward the top. A rectangular pit that may have been a fireplace is built up against the bedrock face.

A 4 ft. high rectangular enclosure inside the stone house at Mystery Walls is presumed to be a fire pit.

A 7 ft. wide gate in the Mystery Walls. The range pole with 12-in. intervals is situated at the foot of the wall on the south side of the gate.

It is situated at about the centre of the "dwelling" and is 3 ft. wide by 4 ft. long.

LATER THAT DAY, Colin Clarke took me to see the petroglyph near Lilly Lake in Waverley—the engraving of a shield that Jack MacNab had discovered. The shield is carved on the top face of a boulder situated in a clearing out on a large section of rock outcrop. It had occurred to Colin that the features on the shield may be connected with Henry Sinclair's visit to the province.

Typical close-up view of the side of the Mystery Walls.

A similar shield was found carved on the face of a stone ledge in Westford, Massachusetts, and is thought to be connected with Sinclair's visit to New England. A version of the story is that Sinclair's party travelled southward along the New England coast to the Merrimack River, just north of Boston, where they landed and spent the winter. In the summer, Sinclair and his party climbed Prospect Hill, located in Westford, to gain a view from its 465-ft. altitude. While in the area, one of Henry Sinclair's lifelong companions, Sir James Gunn, died. The party carved a marker on the face of a stone ledge in his memory. The etching consists of a series of punched holes which outline a Scottish knight with sword and shield. The shield bears similar symbols to the one near Lilly Lake in Waverley.

We also dropped into Admiral's Park to take a quick look at the dolmen perched on the edge of the cliff overlooking Bedford Basin. From the dolmen one can see a tall radio tower on the opposite side of the basin. The tower is near the Mystery Walls. The dolmen site is also on a rock outcrop.

The Mystery Walls site, the dolmen at Admiral's Park, and the shield carving near Lilly Lake all lie on high areas of rock outcropping, commonly called ledges. Clarke says that the location of these sites on the ledges may be no coincidence. The ledges run in a circle around the outskirts of the City of Halifax, encompassing Halifax Harbour and Bedford Basin. "They were used like paved highways by the Indians," Clarke theorizes. "They (the highway-like ledges) may have been introduced to Sinclair's men." Indeed, the notion of their application as natural "paved roads" may have originated with Jack MacNab, himself. Clarke says that MacNab suffered lung damage from toxic fumes while running a cleaning business. His doctor prescribed long fresh air walks as a cure. MacNab began walking the streets and highways but became bored with the repeated scenery. One day, while walking along Rocky Lake Drive, he took to the bush

The engraving of shield on a rock near Lily Lake, Bedford, Nova Scotia. The carving was filled in with white blackboard chalk by the author prior to photographing.

as a diversion. Before long he found himself hiking long distances on the ledges. "It was just like walking the highways, but a lot safer and much more interesting," Clarke explained. It was on these many treks that he began finding oddities such as the Lilly Lake petroglyph.

The Westford Knight

The image known as the Westford Knight, is carved into the face of a stone ledge in Westford, Massachusetts. The site is on the eastern side of Depot Street, 1/2 mi. from the centre of Westford, and an hour's travel from Boston, 1 1/2 mi. west of Route 495, Exit 32.

A modern granite marker beside the ledge in Westford is inscribed as follows:

> *"Prince Henry First Sinclair of Orkney*
> *born in Scotland made a voyage of discovery*
> *to North America in 1398. After*
> *wintering in Nova Scotia he sailed to*
> *Massachusetts and on an inland*
> *expedition in 1399 to Prospect Hill to*
> *view the surrounding countryside,*
> *one of the party died. The*
> *punch-hole armorial effigy which*
> *adorns this ledge is a Memorial to this Knight."*

Look closely at the rock surface. Initially you will notice that a portion of the ledge is painted white in the shape of a shield. Look more closely. Little weatherworn holes outline the shield, while two straight, parallell lines of holes form the sword. On close inspection, other parts of the knightly figure will begin to appear.

The sketch shown at the left will help you visualize the full figure of the Westford Knight.

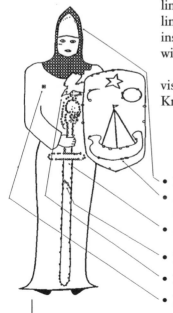

- Hat of a Medieval Knight
- Shield bearing the coat-of-arms of the Gunn family
- Sword, with its pommel, handle, and guard
- Break in the blade indicates death of a Knight
- Falcon
- Rosette, which served as a lance rest

Clarke suggests that the dolmen at Admiral's Park may have been erected by Sinclair's party as a marker in a series of signposts leading from the Shubenacadie River waterway portages to the Mystery Walls. Sinclair's men may have made trips between the Mystery Walls and the Bay of Fundy via the Shubenacadie portages. It would have been natural to portage down to Rocky Lake and follow the rock ledges around to the Mystery Walls.

As for the Lilly Lake petroglyph, it is also on a rock ledge, but rather than being a land marker it may have been carved by an artistic Mi'kmaq, portraying the shield and symbols of one of Sinclair's party. The exposed section of ledge where the shield is situated was probably a temporary stopping place of the Mi'kmaq. There are circular stone fire pits about 4 ft. in diameter near the edges of the clearing. One pit could be very old. Stones partly embedded in moss have lichen growing over their margins. Authenticity of the crest and the fire pits are subject to professional archaeological investigation.

In Clarke's January 1993 letter to Farley Mowat, who was renowned for his reconstruction of the tenth-century Norse voyages of exploration in his book *Westviking*, Clarke gave a description of MacNab's stone house discovery in Waverley and the Mystery Walls of Bayers Lake. He supplied sketches and photographs, asking Mowat's opinion. Mowat wrote back, with this caveat, "They are only impressions because, of course, I haven't seen the sites myself." Mowat says that the sites are clearly of European origin because so far as we know, no aboriginal culture found in this region built structures of this kind. "Why would they have bothered to do so?" Mowat asks. "The only possible reason would have had to be for religious purposes, and there is no indication that they ever wasted time on this sort of monumental 'temple' construction."

Mowat writes that if the sites are European, "and what else could they be?" they would be attributed either to European visitors of the pre-historic discovery period or Europeans of the colonial, or historic era. Of the former, he writes, "I can't find much to suggest this. Early visitors (Celtic, Irish, Welsh or whatever) would have had no reason to build such elaborate and time-consuming structures at some distance inland. The only potential danger from human sources they would have had to deal with would have come from the aboriginals: from landward. They would surely have camped/settled at or on the coast (islands, points, etc.) which were defendable. I can think of no good reason why they would secrete themselves and their structures away from the coasts. And although I have studied every reported ancient European site in North America, I know of none which can be authenticated that would square with these ones. My conclusion is that they are probably not datable to prehistoric discovery period Europeans."

On the speculation of Europeans of the colonial, or historic discovery period, Mowat writes, "My guess is that whoever built these structures was hiding from real or apprehended dangers from seaward, or from the coastal regions. If pre-settlement period, they might have been traders, etc., concealing their presence from competitors. There was certainly fierce and probably lethal competition on the Nova Scotia coasts between Portuguese, French, English, and probably other freebooters and free traders for as much as a century before official settlement began." The use of stones in such large quantities in the Mystery Walls suggested to Mowat that those who built it were in need of a strong defence. Why didn't they build their walls out of wood as there was lots of it? He writes, "The use of stone in such quantities, in a region where there was an ample supply of wood (logs) strongly indicates (to me at any rate) that whoever lived here was willing to spend a hell of a lot of energy erecting walls and structures which would have been at least a lot more defensible than anything made of wood."

Mowat says that the structures could have very well been built by people of the post-settlement period and suggests runaways and outlaws from the Halifax settlement as one possibility. He writes, "There is a close parallel here with the so-called 'Masterless Men' of Newfoundland. In the early colonial period quite large numbers of deserters from naval ships, indentured runaways, and just plain rebels and outlaws, took to the woods where they lived in concealed and sometimes defended little communities, sometimes for generations."

Mowat was inclined to attribute the Mystery Walls to people like the Masterless Men. He says, "It is well known, although historians don't talk about it, that the under-classes in places like early Halifax were abominably treated, and had every incentive to run away and hide from duly constituted, and bloody authority."

Mowat concludes his letter with the comment that "these structures are clearly of considerable historic worth, and should assuredly be protected."

HENRY SINCLAIR has been acknowledged as a member of the Knights Templar, a shadowy order of warrior-monks who reputedly hid an enormous fortune following their abolition by the king of France in

1307. Is there a connection between the Mystery Walls and the Templar treasure that has never been recovered? Is the lost treasure of the Knights Templar hidden somewhere within the confines of these walls? Is there a rich cache stowed away by traders hiding from competitors during the pre-settlement period? Did freebooters holding up in the bush stash away their ill-gotten gains? Were the Mystery Walls the home of rebels and outlaws with fortunes to conceal? Or are the Mystery Walls the home of caches stolen from the rich by the Masterless Men? These are the questions that treasure hunters most assuredly ask.

We may never know. A large twined highway is situated only a few hundred feet to the north of the Mystery Walls. These walls that we have examined may only be a part of a much larger complex lost to the engineer's and contractor's bulldozers and explosives.

CHAPTER SIX

THE MONEY PIT

One day in the spring of 1795 a young man, Daniel McGinnis, was exploring the eastern end of Oak Island, in Mahone Bay on the Atlantic coast of Nova Scotia, when he stumbled upon an unusual clearing in the forest. Old tree stumps were visible among a growth of young trees, and extending across the clearing was the thick limb of a large oak tree from which dangled a ship's tackle block. Below the tackle block lay a circular depression in the ground about 13 ft. in diameter.

Having undoubtedly heard stories of pirates and their buried treasures, and rumours of former pirate activity in Mahone Bay, McGinnis immediately suspected buried bounty and immediately made his discovery known to his two close friends, John Smith, age nineteen, and Anthony Vaughan, age sixteen. The next day the three of them eagerly hurried off to the old clearing.

The tackle block being of great interest, they climbed up on the limb to examine it but it fell to the ground and crumbled into pieces. They then turned their attention to the clearing. Searching about the area, they discovered the remains of a road running from the large oak tree to the western end of the island. Had someone used the road to transport booty to the clearing—perhaps the notorious Captain Kidd? Not to waste time, they hurried back to their homes and returned armed with pickaxes and shovels. They began digging in the depression below which the tackle block had hung, and 2 ft. down they uncovered a layer of carefully laid flagstones. Their excitement heightened. The stones were of a type not indigenous to the island and they figured that they had been brought from Gold River, about 2 mi. north of the island on the mainland.

When the flagstones were removed, the three friends found the mouth of an old shaft or pit that had been refilled. Although the sides of the pit were of hard clay, the soil being removed was loose and easily shovelled without the use of picks; however, pick marks were observed on the sides of the pit as they shovelled downward.

Pirates were known to be a lazy lot and it was common knowledge that they buried their treasures only a few feet underground for easy retrieval. Therefore, McGinnis, Smith, and Vaughan expected to hit the top of a wooden chest each time their shovels bit into the soil, but by the time they had reached a depth of 6 or 7 ft., they began to feel a bit apprehensive.

At a depth of 10 ft., one of the shovels hit wood! "This is it, we've hit the cask," one of the young men shouted with glee. But disappointment quickly followed. What they had struck was a platform of oak logs and not the top of a treasure chest.

The ends of the logs of which the platform was constructed were securely embedded into the sides of the pit. The logs were 6 to 8 in. in diameter, and their outer surface was rotten, giving the impression that they had been there for a very long time.

The trio probably expected to find a treasure chest directly below the platform but on removing the logs they found only a 2-ft. depression caused by soil settlement. However, treasure fever had set in and they returned every day, continuing to dig downward. Finally, at a depth of 25 ft., the work became too difficult and they were forced to abandon the dig.

McGinnis, Smith, and Vaughan believed that someone must have concealed something of extreme value to have gone to the trouble of burying it in excess of 25 ft. So, disappointed but undaunted, they made preparations for future work when help might be available. Before leaving on the final day of digging, they drove wooden sticks into the sides of the pit at the bottom and covered the area with trees and brush.

In the years following the discovery, Daniel McGinnis married and began farming the southwestern end of the island; Anthony Vaughan married and settled on the mainland; and John Smith, who was married before the discovery, built a house near the Money Pit and began farming the eastern end of the island.

OAK ISLAND is a small peanut-shaped parcel of land protected from the open sea by a cluster of small islands. Situated about 40 mi. southwest of Halifax, it is one of some three hundred islands scattered about Mahone Bay on Nova Scotia's Atlantic coast. The island is about a 3/4 mi. long by 1,000 ft. wide at the narrowest section near the centre. The long portion of the island runs in an east to west direction with a small crescent shaped bay called Smith's Cove situated on the north side at the extreme eastern end. The west end of the island is linked to Crandall's Point on the mainland by a narrow causeway constructed in 1965 to transport heavy treasure-digging equipment. The Island, named for beautiful groves of oaks that once shrouded the hills, is now mostly covered with scrub and softwood trees. The east end is sparsely vegetated and severely pocked and scarred from decades of people digging for treasure.

Topographically, Oak Island consists of two oval-shaped hills

Aerial photo of Oak Island taken from 1 mi. above.

about 30 ft. high separated by a swamp and marshy area over the narrow section. Many investigators of the Oak Island mystery believe that the swamp is somehow associated with the Money Pit.

The soil of the island is a hard clay more than 100 ft. in depth, overlying a bedrock of limestone. Deep within the limestone formation, present-day searchers have found what they believe is evidence of man-made workings.

Smith's Cove, it seems, has a very unusual feature. Its beach is artificial! Sometime, long ago, before the discovery of the Money Pit, it was made by man.

The Money Pit lies near the top of the high oval-shaped hill on the east end of the island, 500 ft. from the shore of Smith's Cove. And here, for more than two hundred years men have squandered fortunes and lost their lives in search of buried treasure.

AFTER THE DISCOVERY and initial excavation of the Money Pit, almost a decade elapsed before the dig was resumed. In 1802, a gentleman of financial means by the name of Simeon Lynds from Onslow, Nova Scotia, was in nearby Chester on business and spent an evening with Anthony Vaughan's father. During the course of the evening's conversation, Lynds heard about the discovery. The next day he went over to the island with Vaughan to see the Money Pit for himself and was so enthralled with what he saw that he hurriedly set up a company, signed up investors, and began digging in the summer of the following year.

The Pit had caved in since the work was discontinued in 1795, so the first task was to clean out the mud and debris. This chore was completed with some difficulty but the crew was rewarded by finding the sticks that the three discoverers had driven into the mud, marking where they had stopped digging. The presence of the sticks confirmed that the site had not been tampered with during the eight-year lapse.

Driving downward beyond where McGinnis and his companions had quit, a shovel eventually struck wood. The crew anticipated uncovering a treasure chest, but expectations plunged when all they found was another tier of logs comprising an oak platform similar to the one encountered in 1795.

Ten feet farther down they encountered a layer of charcoal, 10 ft. lower a layer of putty, and much farther down they uncovered an enigmatic object—a flagstone bearing mysterious letters and figures. The stone was about 24 in. long by 16 in. wide and was found with

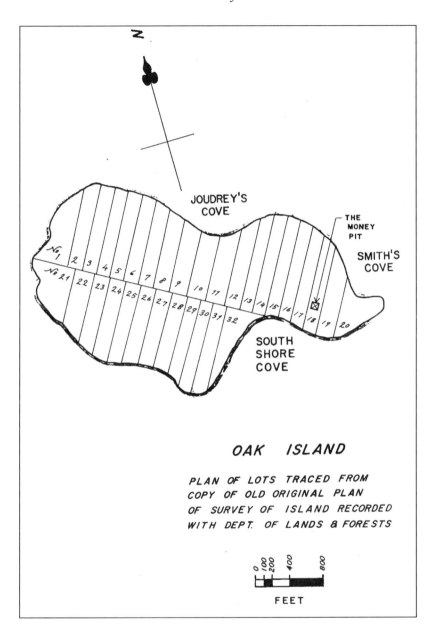

OAK ISLAND

PLAN OF LOTS TRACED FROM
COPY OF OLD ORIGINAL PLAN
OF SURVEY OF ISLAND RECORDED
WITH DEPT. OF LANDS & FORESTS

the figures facing downward. No one in the search party could decipher the stone etchings so it was temporarily cast aside. That strange piece of rock later became one of the most talked about artifacts yet discovered. A presumed copy of the marks and figures found on the stone is given in a book by Edward Rowe Snow titled *True Tales of*

Buried Treasure, published in 1962. According to Snow, a Reverend A. T. Kempton of Cambridge, Massachusetts, claimed that an elderly Irish schoolmaster deciphered the code as, "40 ft. below £2 million are buried."

No water was encountered until the depth reached the 90 ft. level. Here, the bottom of the pit became soggy and water began to ooze from the clay. At 93 ft., water intrusion was becoming a nuisance and the workers found themselves removing one bucket of water for every two of soil. With night approaching, the men probed the mushy bottom of the pit with a crowbar to see if they could strike anything before quitting for the day. This was their standard practice every evening, and on this particular evening, 5 ft. below the bottom of the pit, at a depth of 98 ft., the bar struck a hard, impenetrable material bounded by the sides of the pit.

The searchers suspected that they had finally struck Captain Kidd's treasure and returned home in high spirits. But, when they arrived back at the pit the next morning, they were shocked to find that the shaft which had remained dry throughout all the previous weeks of digging was now filled with about 60 ft. of water.

Discouraged but undaunted, the diggers applied themselves to the task of bailing out the pit with buckets. Although they bailed day and night, their work was useless; the water in the shaft remained at the same level.

As it was approaching haying season, some of the workers had to return home to harvest, so work was temporarily halted. That fall, a group of investors went to see a Mr. Mosher of Newport, Hants County, Nova Scotia, who was considered an expert on the removal of the water. He agreed to set up a pump to get rid of the water for a fee of £80. But when he lowered the pump into the pit to the 90 ft. depth and started it up, the pump burst before the water reached the surface. With winter approaching, the company decided to shut down the project until the next year when an alternative plan could be decided.

The following spring, a shaft was sunk to a depth of 110 ft. just 14 ft. to the southeast of the Money Pit. The plan was to tunnel in under the bottom of the Money Pit and remove the treasure from below. No water at all was encountered on excavating the new shaft and a tunnel was started from the 110 ft. level towards the bottom of the Money Pit. But, when the diggers got to within 2 ft. of the original pit, water began to ooze in small streams from the end of the tunnel. Suddenly, the bank between the end of the tunnel and the

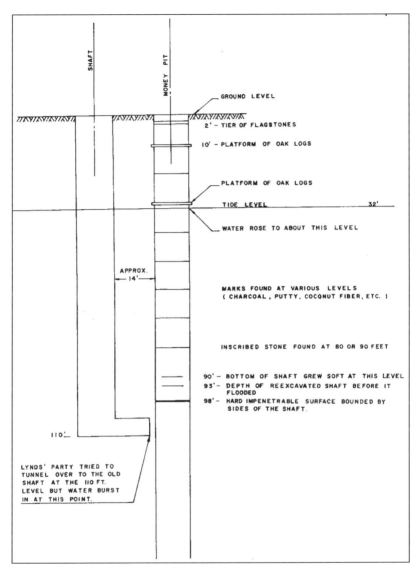

GROUND LEVEL

2' – TIER OF FLAGSTONES

10' – PLATFORM OF OAK LOGS

PLATFORM OF OAK LOGS

TIDE LEVEL   32'

WATER ROSE TO ABOUT THIS LEVEL

APPROX.
— 14'—

MARKS FOUND AT VARIOUS LEVELS
(CHARCOAL , PUTTY, COCONUT FIBER, ETC.)

INSCRIBED STONE FOUND AT 80 OR 90 FEET

90' – BOTTOM OF SHAFT GREW SOFT AT THIS LEVEL
93' – DEPTH OF REEXCAVATED SHAFT BEFORE IT
        FLOODED
98' – HARD IMPENETRABLE SURFACE BOUNDED BY
        SIDES OF THE SHAFT.

110'

LYNDS' PARTY TRIED TO
TUNNEL OVER TO THE OLD
SHAFT AT THE 110 FT.
LEVEL BUT WATER BURST
IN AT THIS POINT.

SHAFT

MONEY PIT

The Money Pit, 1804.

Money Pit collapsed, water burst into the tunnel, and the workmen barely escaped up the shaft with their lives. Within two hours, the new shaft was filled to the 65 ft. level, the same depth of water as in the Money Pit. Further attempts at bailing proved futile and as the company had run out of money, the project was abandoned.

It was not until forty-five years later, in 1849, that another attempt was made to recover Captain Kidd's supposed treasure. A group of businessmen, mostly from Truro, Nova Scotia, formed a company and again tackled the Money Pit.

John Smith had filled in the shafts during the intervening years, so the first job undertaken was to re-excavate the Money Pit. After about two weeks of work, on a Saturday night, the workers reached a depth of 86 ft. But, to their horror, when they returned to the pit the next day, they found 65 ft. of water in the pit. As in 1803, efforts to bail out the pit failed to lower the water by the slightest amount.

Failing to bail out the Money Pit they resorted to drilling, and set up a platform in the pit at the 30 ft. level. A primitive drilling apparatus called a pod auger[1] used for prospecting for coal was set up on the platform and five holes were drilled to a depth of 112 ft.

They lost the only valve sludger[2] they had while attempting to drill the first hole. In a letter to a friend dated June 2, 1862, the manager of operations, Jotham B. McCully, wrote, "Having lost it (the valve sludger) we had only one left, which had, instead of a valve, a ball inside with a pin across the bottom to keep the ball from dropping out. That one would not admit of coin passing into it. It would seem strange that we would not have got another valve sludger, but people who are penny wise and pound foolish sometimes do strange things. I wanted the persons in charge (of the drilling) to send for two or three, but could not prevail on them to do so."

The second drill-hole struck the barrier at the 98 ft. level which the diggers had probed with the crowbar in 1803. It proved to be 6 in. thick and made of spruce. After the auger went through the spruce it dropped a foot and then went through 4 in. of oak, then 20 in. of metal in small pieces, then 8 in. of oak which was thought to be the bottom of one cask and the top of another. The auger went then through another 20 in. of metal, the same as before, 4 in. of oak, 6 in. of spruce, and 7 ft. of "worked clay" before hitting hard clay that had never been disturbed. The men were able to discern that the metal was "in pieces" from the sound that the auger made as it passed through and the ease with which it went through. But the only evidence of treasure the auger brought up were three pieces of metal resembling links from an ancient watch chain. McCully stated that the metal pieces were gold.

Another of the drill-holes struck the barrier at 98 ft., dropped 18 in., and scraped the side of an oak cask evidenced by splinters of oak similar to what might be brought up from the side of an oak stave. McCully also mentioned bringing up a brown fibrous substance "closely resembling the husk of a coconut." Further borings added nothing more.

The next summer, in 1850, the company sank a shaft 10 ft. northwest of the Money Pit to a depth of 109 ft. without striking water. But when they tunnelled towards the bottom of the Money Pit to reach the casks, they again barely escaped with their lives when water burst into the tunnel and the new shaft filled up with 45 ft. of water in twenty minutes.

It was around this time that someone in the search party noticed that the water in the shafts was salt, and that it rose and fell about 18 in. with the tides. The water levels in the Money Pit and the two shafts were also observed to be the same as the mean tide levels of the bay.

Why was water encountered in the Money Pit but not in the shafts dug in 1804 and 1850? the searchers asked. Was it possible that the Money Pit was connected by a tunnel to the sea?

A small stream of water had been observed flowing out of the bank on the shore of Smith's Cove at low tide. Did this water flow from the Money Pit? The search party set about searching the beach.

Shovelling away some of the sand and gravel on the beach exposed a bed of a brown fibrous plant that was later confirmed to be coconut fibre. The fibre bed was about 2 in. thick and stretched for 145 ft. along the shore from low to high water marks. Below this and of the same length and width, they found a 4 or 5 in. thick bed of eel grass. Underlying the eel grass was a dense mass of beach stones, free from sand and gravel. The beach was obviously artificial!

To make a full investigation possible, the searchers built a coffer-dam of rock and clay around the cove to keep back the tides. When the dam was completed and the area free of water, they discovered that the original clay had been removed and replaced with beach stones. Five well-constructed box drains made out of stone rested on this excavation. The entrances of these drains were widely separated along the full length of the excavation at low tide and converged like the fingers of a hand to a common point near the shore. Both the excavation and the drains sloped downward from low water to the shore.

Work of digging up the construction was carried out from low water towards the shore but only a portion of the drainage system was uncovered. An unusually high tide carried the dam away. However, enough had been observed to estimate where the drains converged at the shore and two shafts were sunk a short distance inland in an effort to intercept and plug the tunnel.

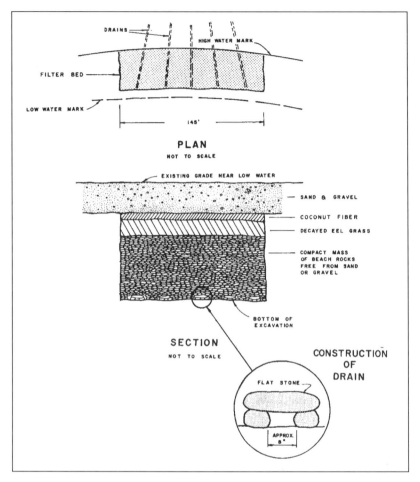

Findings at Smith's Cove excavation, 1850.

The search party dug the first shaft to a depth of 75 ft. without striking water. Then they moved 12 ft. to the south and dug another shaft encountering a rush of water when a rock was removed at a depth of 35 ft. Water rose in the hole to tide level within minutes which proved they had struck the tunnel. In an attempt to block the flow of water in the tunnel they drove wood stakes into the bottom of the shaft and partially filled it with soil.

Hoping that they had blocked the water channel, the searchers attempted to bail the Money Pit. They succeeded in lowering the water slightly but not enough to be of any use. Again they tried to reach the bottom of the Money Pit by lateral tunnelling. This time they sunk a shaft slightly south of their first one on the same side of the Money Pit to a depth of 112 ft. But, as with their first procedure that failed them earlier and had failed the Lynds's party in 1804, they were driven out when water burst into the tunnel and flooded the shaft.

The following year (1851) the same group tried to raise more money to continue the search but investors were discouraged and the operation came to an end. A lot of money had been spent without recovering a single coin.

The discovery of oak casks, however, the artificial beach, and the flood tunnel stirred up a lot of interest and enthusiasm, and in the spring of 1861 a new syndicate, also of Truro, called the Oak Island Association, was formed. The new group put together a work force of sixty-three men and thirty-three horses and was convinced that it would be able to drain the Money Pit and bring up the "treasure" with an army of this size.

The workers cleaned out the Money Pit which had caved in over the past decade and recribbed it to a depth of 88 ft. At this point the crew stopped digging since the clay soil below appeared to be blocking any serious water intrusion from the yet to be located flood tunnel.

Presuming that the flood tunnel ran straight to where the drains converged on the shore, they excavated a 120 ft. deep shaft at a point 25 ft. east of the Money Pit but missed the water channel. Abandoning, for the moment, further efforts to intercept the water tunnel they resorted to an old approach.

Not having learned from the failures of previous years, the workers tried to reach the vault from below by lateral tunnelling. They sank another shaft 18 ft. west of the Money Pit to a depth of 118 ft. They then drove a tunnel 3 ft. wide by 4 ft. high for a distance of 17 ft. towards the Money Pit before water broke in. Then they tried to reach the supposed treasure casks by tunnelling from the bottom of the first 120 ft. deep shaft. That also failed as it began to fill with water. A desperate attempt was then made to stem the rising water. They rigged four 70-gallon bailing casks over the Money Pit and the other two shafts, and the men and horses worked in shifts for several days. This operation progressed rather well and almost succeeded in draining the pits, but it was hampered when the tunnel connecting the 118 ft. deep shaft choked up with soft clay causing the diabolical water to rise once again in the Money Pit.

Two men were sent down to clear the mud from the connecting tunnel but half-way through the tunnel, they were stunned by a thunderous crash above them. A wall of mud pitched forward with enormous momentum. Terrified, the men ran for their lives and barely escaped being entombed. And then, plank by plank, the Money Pit cribbing fell downward, just as if the bottom had fallen out of the pit, and all the structures above, including the sought-after treasure vaults were swallowed up by the depths below.

Samuel C. Fraser, a member of the Oak Island Association, recalled the catastrophe in a 1895 letter to A. S. Lowden, then manager of a search group: "I was sent down to clean out the Money Pit, but before going into it I examined the 118 ft. pit and tunnel, which was then nearly finished. At the end of the tunnel I saw every sign of the cataclysm that was about to take place and I refused to go into the Money Pit.... When the pit fell down I was there.... There went down 10,000 ft. of lumber, board measure, the cribbing of the old Money Pit." He described the water in the pit as "boiling like a volcano." The Money Pit had collapsed and lay in ruins and whatever treasure it may have held disappeared into the soupy bowels of the earth somewhere below Oak Island.

The collapse of the Money Pit signalled an end to sixty-six years of significant discoveries since the three young men set out to unearth what they supposed was the treasure of the notorious Captain Kidd.

However, the quest for untold riches at Oak Island did not end. Numerous well-financed expeditions followed. They dug shaft after shaft and drilled hundreds of holes into the island, desperately seeking clues to what lay below.

IN 1897, A SEARCH GROUP called the Oak Island Treasure Company, organized by Frederick Blair, finally discovered the flood channel at the Money Pit. At 111 ft. down in the pit the crew discovered a well-defined 2$^{1/2}$ ft. wide opening in the east wall which they determined was the flood tunnel outlet. The sides and top of the tunnel were cut from solid clay. The sides were vertical, the top horizontal, and the whole tunnel was filled with beach stones, gravel, and sand. Seawater gushed from the opening with great force. Several accounts give the height of the tunnel as 4 ft. but Captain John Welling, director of operations for the company, notes that the full height couldn't be ascertained due to the volume of water gushing from the tunnel. A bird's bone, a chip of wood, and a piece of bark taken from the sand and gravel confirmed a connection with the sea.

Further exploration detected a cement chamber far below the

collapsed bottom of the Money Pit. Planning to locate the casks lost in the 1861 collapse of the pit which were thought to be somewhere around the 118 ft. level, the Oak Island Treasure Company set up pumps which held the water down to the 100 ft. level while several exploratory drill holes were put down from a platform at 90 ft. The first hole bored through 5 in. of well-preserved oak at the 126 ft. level (measured from the ground surface) and then struck an iron obstruction which could not be drilled through. Surprised by this encounter, Blair and Captain Welling ordered the drillers to shift a little to one side and try again. They drilled a foot away from the first hole, and this time slipped past the obstruction at 126 ft. Continuing downward, the drill struck soft stone or cement at a depth of 153' 8" which was 7 in. thick overlaying 5 in. of solid oak. Below the oak was a 1$^{1/2}$ to 2 in. gap followed by what William Chappell, company board member, described in an affidavit as "a substance the character of which no person would attempt to state." Chappell goes on to say: "After considerable twisting of the auger on the substance, it was carefully withdrawn and the borings brought up therewith were preserved by Mr. Putnam (T. Perley Putnam, company manager). The drill was then again put down when we found we were apparently on soft metal that could be moved slightly thereby forming a crevice or space into which the drill, when in alignment, would drop and stick and wedge." They experienced considerable difficulty getting down through the metal which the drillers thought consisted of metal in bars for the first 4 in. followed by metal in pieces or coin, but they managed to bore down through 2' 8" where the drill struck a substance similar to that first encountered. The drill jammed and stopped on this material and no effort was made to go through it.

A third drill hole struck wood at 122 ft. and cement at 153 ft. The drill touched wood on one side which extended down about 4 ft. and cement on the other which continued down an additional 3 ft. to about 160 ft. Drilling down below the cement, the drill struck an iron barrier at 171 ft.—immediately recognized by its sound at the surface. Two hours or more of drilling only pierced the iron 1/4 in., and the attempt to drill through it was abandoned.

The borings that were brought up from a little below 154 ft. and given to Putnam consisted of oak chips, coconut fibre, and a very small mysterious artifact that still haunts people today.

Putnam personally removed and cleaned the borings from the drill and the samples were never out of his possession until they were examined by a physician, Dr. A. E. Porter, at the Courthouse in

Amherst. The doctor studied the borings with a powerful magnifying glass within the presence of thirty-five or more people. Blair's lawyer, Reginald V. Harris writes: "The strange fibre attracted his attention. Under the glass it appeared in the form of a compact ball about the size of a grain of rice, with fuzz or short hair on the surface. After working with it for some minutes he got it flattened out, when it had every appearance of being a small piece of parchment, upon which was written in black ink, characters that appeared to represent parts of the letters "ui", "vi," or "wi." It was afterwards sent to experts in Boston and by them pronounced to be parchment, upon which there was writing in India ink, written with a quill pen."

It was during their drilling operation that the Oak Island Treasure Company were the first to detect another flood tunnel. A couple of more holes were drilled which didn't reveal any significant additional information about the nature of the cement cask, but one of the holes appeared to intercept a channel from which water was pumped out at a rate of about 400 gallons per minute. This suggested a second water tunnel probably from the south shore!

Excited by the discovery of a cement cask that might contain bars of gold and silver, coins and jewels, and possibly very important and valuable historical documents, the company devised a plan to recover the treasure by sinking a shaft 175 ft. to 200 ft. deep and tunnelling to a point below the iron obstruction at the 171 ft. level in the Money Pit. This new shaft was to be used to drain the pit by pumping, thus allowing the diggers to reach the cement vault.

They sunk a shaft about 40 ft. south of the Money Pit but were driven out when a large volume of salt water broke in at the 70 ft. level from an old shaft of the 1860s. The water rose to tide level.

Determined to reach the supposed enormous treasure they tried again. This time they selected a spot about 80 ft. south of the Money Pit, but they were again defeated when at 160 ft., salt water again broke into the shaft from a seam of sand. Four more shafts using the same approach were excavated and all ended in failure due to unsafe soil conditions, boulders, or water intrusion.

Very discouraged but still determined to reach the cache, they made a last-ditch effort to cope with the water entering the Money Pit. The workers ran tests to see if the tunnel from Smith's Cove was really clogged. They filled one of the abandoned shafts with water pumped from the shore, and soon the muddy water fell back to sea level. But, to their dismay, it showed up at three widely separated points near the low tide line of the south shore. This confirmed that there was a second water channel (natural or man-made). They found similar results when water was pumped into the Money Pit and again when red dye was poured into the pit. A fourth test consisted of lowering the water in the Money Pit and letting it settle until it was clear. Then, they set off a charge of dynamite near one of the south shore inlets. In a short time, muddy water came through to the pit.

A CLUE THAT THERE might be a vault in the limestone formation beneath the island came in 1938 when Edwin H. Hamilton, Associate Professor of Engineering at New York University, took over the search. After spending considerable time and effort exploring tunnels beneath the island, he deepened a shaft near the Money Pit of a former expedition to 167 ft. where he struck a 24 ft. thick layer of limestone bedrock. He drilled down through the limestone to a depth below 200 ft. and brought up oak chips, suggesting that he may have struck a man-made structure.

Proof of a cavern, natural or man-made, beneath the Money Pit came in 1955 when George Greene of Corpus Christi, Texas, who represented five large oil companies, joined the search. Greene, a burly cigar-chewing petroleum engineer, complete with wide-brimmed Stetson and cowboy boots, remarked that this would be the first time oil drilling methods would be applied on Oak Island in "the search for the gold," and that the Texas backers were willing to spend "any amount of money" if the drilling results were encouraging. He told newspaper reporters, "If we don't hit a concrete vault with this drilling we'll pack up and I'll head for South America and an oil drilling job." As a compensation in the event of failure, Greene advised the press that there was a strong possibility of Hollywood making a movie about Oak Island and said, "So if we don't find the treasure we may get our money back with the movie rights."

Greene drilled four holes with a 4-in. core drill in the Money Pit area and reported finding platforms every 10 ft. down to about the 112 ft. level. "Below that there is nothing but cavity. The drills just drop right through. We went to 180 ft. in one hole before we found the bottom of [the] cavity," Greene reported. He then pumped 100,000 gallons of water into the cavity to try and determine its size, but it disappeared with no trace of where it went. This was the first time anyone had proved the existence of a cavern, natural or man-made, beneath the Money Pit.

Further confirmation of an subterranean cavern was provided by Robert R. Dunfield, a long-experienced petroleum geologist of

Canoga Park, California, and a graduate of the University of California at Los Angeles (UCLA) who took over the operation in 1965. After excavating for the south shore flood tunnel but finding no trace of it, he turned to the Money Pit. With huge equipment, he dug a hole nearly 140 ft. deep by 100 ft. in diameter and ripped out most of the old cribbing from earlier shafts and tunnels. Throughout the dig, the project was besieged by mechanical breakdowns and heavy rains. The sides of the big pit kept caving in during the storms and one day's work was cancelled out by another day or two of rain.

So, after more than two months of sluggish digging, Dunfield refilled the huge hole to provide a solid soil platform from which a drilling operation could be conducted. Working from the soil platform, Dunfield drilled a series of 6-in. holes to almost 190 ft. In several of the holes, he encountered the cavity or cavern that Greene had discovered in 1955. The drill struck a 24-in. layer of limestone at depths between 140 and 142 ft. and then dropped down into a 40-ft. void to bedrock! In April 1966, Dunfield called it quits and returned to California. The expedition had cost him an estimated $131,000.

The current search at the Money Pit is managed by former Miami, Florida, building contractor, Daniel Blankenship, who took over when Dunfield dropped out in 1966.

At first, Blankenship commuted on a seasonal basis between Florida and Nova Scotia, spending the winters at home in Miami with his wife and family. But, finally, in 1975, he moved them to the island where he built his present home.

From the outset, Blankenship envisaged a careful and comprehensive drilling program to be followed by a well thought out excavation. To this end he sought a backer and teamed up with David Tobias, a well-established Montreal businessman who was able to attract wealthy investors.

Tobias formed Triton Alliance Limited in April 1969 with himself as president and Blankenship as director of field operations. But before the company was formed the two men carried out a substantial search. In 1966 they deepened an excavation Dunfield had made while searching for a south shore flood tunnel. At a depth of 60 ft. they uncovered an "ancient hand-wrought nail and something resembling a "nut or washer." At 90 ft. down they found "a layer of round granite stones the size of a man's head." The rocks were laying in a pool of stagnant water and Blankenship felt that there was a high probability that they had intercepted a portion of a south shore flood system. They spent several months trying to crib and deepen the shaft until the work was abandoned when soil collapsed into the hole.

In 1967 Blankenship dug up sections of the beach at Smith's Cove and found coconut fibre and the remains of the old drainage system. Other discoveries under the beach included a pair of wrought iron scissors of three-hundred-year-old pattern, a chiselled heart-shaped stone and an old set square which metallurgists dated prior to 1780.

In 1970 Triton Alliance constructed a 400 ft. long cofferdam around the perimeter of Smith's Cove and 50 ft. further out to sea than those of earlier days. It was destroyed by an Atlantic storm but its construction yielded a significant discovery.

A large U-shaped wooden structure was uncovered below low tide. It was made of several large 2 ft. thick logs 30 to 65 ft. long. The logs were notched at 4-ft. intervals and a Roman numeral was carved beside each notch. Each numeral was different. The notches had been bored and several contained 2 in. thick wooden dowels. The notches and dowels were thought to have secured cross pieces between the logs. Experts concluded that the structure was an ancient wharf or slipway or the remains of workings used in the con-struction of an original cofferdam built to hold back the tides while the flood system was being constructed.

A lot of Blankenship's and Tobias's work has consisted of exploratory drilling from which some significant clues have been uncovered. They learned from drilling near the Money Pit that there are caverns or tunnels in the bedrock far below the island with ceil-ings of wood planks or logs. These caverns were discovered about 40 ft. down in the bedrock which was found to begin about 160 ft. below the ground surface or about 170 ft. below the "original ground." [3]

During the drilling operations, pieces of china, cement, wood, charcoal, metal and oak buds were brought up in locations varying from 170 ft. to 222 ft. below the original ground surface. On striking tunnels or caverns, the drill would first cut through 30 or 40 ft. of bedrock and then hit two layers of wood, each several inches thick, separated by a thin layer of clay. The drill would then drop down through a void between 6 to 8 ft. deep before again striking bedrock. Tobias told me that wood brought up from these deep levels was carbon dated at 1575 plus or minus eighty-five years.[4] When Tobias was questioned about the unusual discovery of wood and cavities down in the bedrock, he said, "The oak samples were quite under-standably found at the 200 ft. level. No one would have built a vault above the bedrock where it could be easily reached."

One drill hole became a shaft which stirred up a whirlpool of public attention. The shaft, designated Borehole 10-X and situated about 180 ft. northeast of the Money Pit, began as just another 6-in. diameter drill hole but the cavities encountered encouraged Triton to concentrate its efforts on this spot.

In the initial probe, they encountered 5 ft. deep cavities at 140 and 160 ft. depths, bedrock at 180 ft., and another cavity at 230 ft. They brought up small quantities of metal from the 165 ft. level which encouraged Triton to enlarge the hole to 27 in. in diameter down to the lowest cavity at 230 ft. In drilling the wider hole, pieces of wood, metal, chain, and broken wire were brought up. The hole filled to sea level with salt water and pieces of bird bones, seashells, and glass came to the surface suggesting a connection with the flood system at Smith's Cove.

Triton lowered an underwater remote-controlled television camera down into the 230 ft. deep cavity while Blankenship watched a closed-circuit monitor in a nearby shack. Nothing but "snow" first appeared on the screen but suddenly there appeared what seemed to be the faint outlines of three chests, one with a handle on the end and a curved top, a pick-axe, and three logs lying on the floor of the cavern. The next view showed what appeared to be a human hand which was half-clenched and severed at the wrist. It hung suspended for a few minutes in front of the camera lens until it was accidentally struck by the camera and dropped out of site. The camera also picked up what appeared to be a human body slumped in a sitting position against a wall of the chamber.

Bore Hole 10-X was later increased to a diameter of about 8 ft. and extended downward with the anticipation of finding a tunnel to the Money Pit. The results were disappointing. The cavities at 140 ft. and 160 ft. were found to be natural, and the bottom void at 230 ft. was indicated by sonar surveying equipment to have no tunnel leading to it and was therefore assumed to be natural.

No additional shafts of the magnitude of Bore Hole 10-X have been excavated but Blankenship and Tobias hope to one day raise sufficient funds to enable a major dig at the Money Pit.

SEVERAL YEARS AGO, I took a boat jaunt around Oak Island as a guest of the tour vessel's captain. Copies of my first book on the mystery, *The Oak Island Quest*, were prominently stacked on the tour captain's gift shop counter, back at the marina. Perhaps to protect me from a barrage of questions or to ensure he could speak without interruptions since he was giving the tour talk, the skipper decided not to introduce me as the author. So, I sat with the guests and listened to the Oak Island story as if I had been hearing it for the first time.

We had rounded the eastern tip of the island and were passing the south shore when the skipper said, "And, then they (those who constructed the Money Pit) excavated another tunnel to the south shore. During winters when the water on this side of the shore is frozen, I have seen air holes in the ice caused by the water tunnel."

This was a new piece of information for me, supporting the existence of a second flood tunnel. I recalled confirmation of a water channel to the south shore made by dye tests carried out by a treasure expedition in the late 1800s. I made a mental note to discuss the matter with Triton but it wasn't until sometime in 1992 when I was writing my second book about the island, *Oak Island Gold*, that I addressed the tour captain's statement.

Dan Blankenship confirmed that he had witnessed these holes in the ice. He had noted four holes out on the ice off the south shore in the winter of 1980. The holes were about 150 ft. apart and thought to have been formed by warmer water rising from the sea bottom. Blankenship had caused a circulation of water at that time under the vicinity of the Money Pit while pumping water from nearby shafts. Geologists were told about the phenomenon and voiced the opinion that there was a link between the Money Pit and these mysterious openings in the ice.

By pure coincidence, I later ran into a diver who had been sent down with others to explore the sea bottom in search of the source of these holes in the ice. "We found circular vertical holes some distance out on the bottom ... below low tide," he said. "I laid down beside one of them and stuck my arm in. I reached down as far as I could but there was no bottom." On further questioning, he said, "The holes aren't natural. I've done a lot of diving but I've never seen anything like that before. They're definitely man-made."

If what the diver told me can be taken as true, the magnitude of the original works in and surrounding the Money Pit may be almost beyond belief.

CHAPTER SEVEN

NOLAN'S CROSS

I t was low tide when the bow of the small aluminum boat scraped the rocky bottom of Joudrey's Cove, on the northern side of Oak Island. I was seated in the middle and hopped out to lighten the load and pull the boat up onto the beach. Frederick G. Nolan, Nova Scotia Land Surveyor and owner of a large central portion of the island, tilted up the outboard motor and tied the bow rope to a boulder near high water. The two-hundred-year search for the elusive treasure had taken a bizarre turn and I was there to investigate a strange phenomenon.

Nolan, who has been involved in the search for almost forty years, was about to go public with what he said would "amaze the world." He had made a most unusual discovery and felt that it should be verified by a civil engineer before disclosure to the press. So, on Nolan's behest, I had driven down from Halifax, loaded the boat with necessary survey equipment to include transit, tripods, range poles, and electronic distance measuring equipment, and struck off with Nolan for the island.

At this point, I had a well-conceived notion of what Nolan had discovered. Rather than just phoning me and saying, "Will you go over to the island and conduct a survey of a new discovery?" Nolan had used a more subtle approach. He was unsure of what my response would have been. I might have asked a lot of questions. His answers, although true, might have sounded ridiculous. I might have dragged my feet on providing any help.

So, about a month earlier he phoned and arranged to meet for coffee. In a small shop overlooking Halifax Harbour, he presented a colour photograph of a large sandstone boulder about 4 ft. in diameter. The rock resembled the profile of a human skull!

After allowing me a few minutes to study the photograph, Nolan gave me a brief overview. The skull-shaped rock, which he had dubbed the "Head Stone" was situated among several large granite boulders that formed a pattern which provided a clue to where the "treasure" was buried. These boulders were survey markers although they gave no appearance of serving that purpose. "This was intentional," Nolan said. They were not hand-shaped in any way, just natural rocks, and they were large. "You could be leaning against one and never recognize it as a survey monument," Nolan said. Nolan explained that the rock survey markers were intended to appear natural so that no one would "get tipped off" and go searching for the treasure. They were only supposed to be meaningful to the people who put them there but were also meaningful to him because when he ran lines through unquestionably artificial attachments in rocks, such as anchor bolts, he intercepted these markers.

What Nolan was telling me didn't seem incredible because he had initiated me a week earlier when we had met to discuss something that he said "might be of considerable interest to me." He said that he had made a breakthrough and was considering going forward with an excavation. I was in the throes of writing a new book on Oak Island and eager for new information.

Nolan didn't tell me what his "breakthrough" was but laid the groundwork. He told of finding survey markers that looked natural to the layman, although they proved to be man-made. For years he had run survey lines through points he had found, and one line would frequently intersect another. "I would find two markers and project a line through them and find a third but at that time it didn't make any sense," he said. However, as time went on the pieces of the puzzle began to fall into place.

After finding two or three survey markers in one location and two or three in another, he ran lines between them in all directions. "I would go to sleep at night wondering what I might learn by joining one point to another. Then I would go out to the island the next day and survey for the answer," Nolan reminisced. He said that when he took measurements between markers, he was looking for a "pattern." "I felt that all those markers had to mean something," Nolan said. "The trick was to discover or figure out the pattern they represented."

Now, after years of investigation, Nolan claimed to have discovered a system to all the markers he surveyed—they form a mathematical equation that involves not only trigonometry but, strangely, symbolism as well. That, he told me at our second meeting, is where the Head Stone applies!

Nolan said that the Head Stone was laying on its side when he discovered it. The side or face of the stone was slightly slanted with the top portion, or head, exposed. He dug it up with a backhoe and photographed it. At that point it meant nothing more to him than just another rock to be examined. But it was a rock that shouldn't have been there. It was composed of sandstone and bore glacial striation lines indicating it once was part of a bedrock formation. Sandstones are not indigenous to the island. Of course, this could have been a fluke of nature, but as Nolan later discovered, it wasn't.

The Head Stone.

I had no reason to doubt Nolan's claim to finding survey markers that might relate to the Oak Island puzzle. Over the four decades of Nolan's search, press releases had given a smattering of details which included a noteworthy discovery believed to be an old stone surveyor's monument. Nolan described the monument as being "similar to the type used by surveyors today." He verified that the stone was man-made by having it examined and analyzed by a geologist, Robert Grantham, who reported that, "The upper 6 or 7 in. of rock have been exposed to the weather for quite some time. There were lichens growing on the upper 4 in. and below that are marks made by vegetation growth in the soil which surrounded the rock." He also reported that, "The rock was found on end. This is not a natural stable resting position for a rock of this shape." It is square in cross section with two sides smooth or natural and the other two sides rough as if cut by a chisel. Burn marks are visible suggesting that heat was applied to cut the rock.

On winding up our second meeting where I was introduced to the Head Stone, Nolan proposed that I transport my survey equipment over to the island to conduct a survey of a few of the markers. "I needed something of a substantial nature to show," he said. "I needed something that people would be able to understand and relate to, and now I have it." He said that he wanted an engineer to check some of his measurements and verify his findings, now that he was prepared to go public with an outstanding discovery. He said he would have the press on hand while I conducted my survey. They could take pictures and he was prepared to answer questions.

As we shook hands on leaving the coffee shop, I had asked Nolan what the Head Stone and the granite boulders that he said were survey markers "were really all about." Nolan had replied, "The answer must be supported by the evidence. If I told someone what the answer to the puzzle is, they would think I was crazy."

On the day Nolan agreed to survey his new discovery, we met at his museum on Crandall's Point before crossing over to his property on the island. While we were chatting in the museum's reception room, Nolan opened his attaché case and handed me a plot plan showing the configuration of one of the most ancient and symbolic image known to man—a cross! The configuration resembled a giant Latin cross or crucifix. Each arm of the cross was 360 ft. in length and the total length of the stem was 867 ft. The ends of the arms and the top and bottom of the stem each terminated at a circle marked by the word "cone," and the stem was also divided by a circle marked "cone" situated 293 ft. from the bottom. The centre of the cross (where the arms meet the stem) was marked "headstone."

At the left-hand bottom corner of the plot was a diagram of a cone entitled "cone boulder size" indicating that the cones represented rocks; the cone was shown as 8 ft. wide at the base and 9 ft. tall.

The cross on the plot plan was almost perfectly proportioned. Within 2 ft., the stem from the Head Stone to the bottom (or the

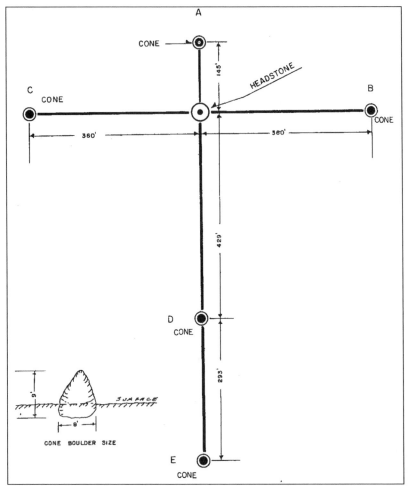

Nolan's plot plan, almost perfectly proportioned.

"body") was twice the length of either arm. Within 3 ft., the stem from the Head Stone to the top (or "top") was five times the length of the body and twice the distance of the cone at the bottom of the body to the "divider." These almost numerically even ratios of body to arms and top to body suggested that what Nolan had discovered was not a fluke of nature.

We were waiting for the press as I studied Nolan's plot plan and worked out the impressive ratios on a pocket calculator. The meeting had been arranged for 1:00 P.M., but Nolan had been held up in traffic and was half an hour late. The press arrived in the meantime, gave Nolan fifteen minutes grace, and left. We assumed that the news

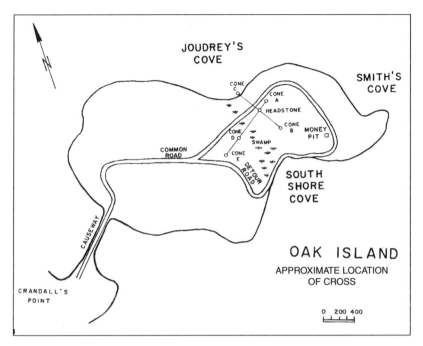

This diagram of Oak Island shows the size and location of Nolan's Cross.

people had gone for a quick lunch and would be back, so we waited. And while we waited Nolan reminisced.

He first became interested in Oak Island in 1958 after reading a book, *The Oak Island Mystery*, by Reginald V. Harris. Harris's definitive history of the early searches sparked Nolan's curiosity and zeal for adventure. Nolan paid Harris several visits as their offices were only a few blocks apart, and after discussing the mystery at length with the author, he resolved to try and recover the long sought treasure.

But he was obliged to wait in the wings as there was a line-up of treasure hunters waiting to take a crack at the Money Pit. However, he didn't stand idly by while waiting. There was much he wanted to investigate—clues that might help in locating the treasure. Nolan talked about a few. There was an old equilateral triangle of hand-placed beach stones about 12 to 14 in. in diameter near the south shore about 300 ft. from the Money Pit. The triangle measured about 10 ft. per side and a line of stones running from the base to the apex pointed towards the Money Pit. It was discovered in 1897, but no one knew its purpose and whether it was part of the original

Money Pit construction or placed by an earlier search party. The entire figure is said to have resembled a giant sextant.

A white granite boulder with a drill hole in it lay about 50 ft. north of the Money Pit and another near the shore of Smith's Cove and about 400 ft. from the first. Both boulders were marked with drill holes 2 in. deep by 1 1/4 in. in diameter which were obviously man-made. These drill-holes were thought to have been made by the builders of the Money Pit complex and to be part of some type of marking system in relation to the stone triangle on the south shore.

Three piles of stones formed the corners of a triangle in the shape of an arrowhead. They were situated on the top of the hill above the swamp that occupies the centre of the island. The arrow-like formation pointed directly to the centre of the swamp. What did these oddities signify? They were clues that indicated that "There was more to the picture than the Money Pit," Nolan recalled. "I had the feeling that the island had to be looked on as a whole. That's when I decided to conduct a survey and tie everything in."

Accordingly, between 1961 and 1962, Nolan laid out a grid over the entire island, referencing all relevant markers. It was a large pro-ject for a speculative venture, and indicates Nolan's optimism. Dozens of lines, some thousands of feet long, were cut through brush and heavily wooded areas and twenty-three concrete survey monu-ments were established, complete with numbered bronze discs for accurate positioning of a transit or theodolite. It was a thorough and labour-intensive survey and, significantly, objects that would later be lost (the stone triangle near the south shore was destroyed by a search party in the mid-1960s) were referenced to the grid.

On completing the survey, Nolan made an unsuccessful bid to lease Oak Island and continue the dig at the Money Pit, but he was successful in purchasing about a quarter of the island adjacent to and west of the Money Pit. This property contained Joudrey's Cove, some high and dry land and most of the swamp to which the arrow-like formation of the stone piles pointed.

Nolan had for some time suspected that there might be a water-tight vault somewhere else on the island with a shaft running down-ward. It was now time to test out his theory and he embarked on an intensive search of his lands.

Nolan was surprised at what he found. His property, which extends entirely across the island on the east side, contained numer-ous markers and objects that he believes are related to the original works. He discovered rocks with round holes bored or chiselled into them and some had pieces of metal inserted into the surfaces. He found ring bolts set in granite boulders. He dug up pieces of old hand-cut wood which he believes are from an ancient treasure chest. He also found beach stones, bits of old wood, and metal beneath the swamp, and pieces of wood and rocks that he believes are survey monuments associated with the island's puzzle.

Nolan referenced all his findings to monuments on his grid system and began drawing lines through points and extrapolating them in search of mathematical relationships. Sometimes, when he would run a line between two previously discovered markers, he would prolong that line and discover another marker. A configuration was beginning to form and he knew that he was on to something big. It was in the process of surveying and drafting the locations of his findings that the large Latin cross formed by the Head Stone and cone-shaped granite boulders one day revealed itself on the drawing board. It was this cross that he wanted me to survey and confirm the measurements that he had made.

The press had not returned by 1:45 P.M., so we backed Nolan's pickup truck down to the water's edge, unloaded his 12 ft. aluminum boat, loaded on the surveying equipment and headed out for Oak Island and the "cross."

On the way over to the island, Nolan apologized for the inconvenience of travelling by boat. "You'd think it was fifty years ago," he remarked, nodding in the direction of the one-lane causeway connecting Crandall's Point on the mainland to the western end of the Island. It was built by Robert Dunfield in 1965 to transport heavy excavation equipment to the Money Pit and has been in use as a roadway ever since, except for Nolan! After the causeway was finished, an armed guard was posted at the entrance to prevent Nolan from using it. "Dunfield himself used to sit out there with a rifle and threaten to shoot me if I tried to cross his causeway," he told me.

Nolan retaliated the following year (1966) by purchasing land at Crandall's Point that abutted the entrance to the causeway. He then barricaded it. This created a stalemate which was temporarily solved in 1968 by a six-month agreement in which Dan Blankenship, who had taken over the operation of the Money Pit from Dunfield, paid Nolan $1,000 to cross the Crandall's Point land. The agreement was later revised with Nolan acquiring a few shares in the Money Pit operation in exchange for surveying on drilling work and granting Blankenship and his new partner David Tobias a right-of-way over the road to the pit (the road to the Money Pit crossed Nolan's land).

But the agreement was short-lived. It was annulled in 1969 when Triton Alliance was formed. Each side accused the other of breach of contract.

Nolan then again blocked off the causeway entrance, forcing Triton to construct a bypass road to it. In retaliation, Triton chained off the causeway where it meets the island thus preventing Nolan access to his property in the centre of the island. Now Nolan was forced to take a boat from Crandall's Point to Joudrey's Cove where his property fronts on a section of beach on the north side of the island. As a counter move, Nolan chained off the road to the Money Pit that crosses his property. With no way to drive out to the Pit, Triton eventually built its own road which took a detour around Nolan's land.

As we reached Joudrey's Cove, the conversation returned to the cross. "There is the first cone," Nolan said, pointing to a large conical granite boulder about the size of a compact automobile and situated between high and low tides at about 40 ft. below the high water mark of the shore. Nolan explained that this boulder is the cone lettered "C" on the left end of the arm of the Cross shown on his plot plan. Nolan pointed out that the body or stem of the cross straddles the swamp with the top cone and Head Stone on the east side and the two bottom cones on the west, all on dry land; the stem of the cross runs in a northeast direction from the bottom to the top; the arms are at right angles to the stem and run southeast from the cone on Joudrey's Cove.

After giving me a general rundown on the layout, Nolan took me for a tour of the Cross. We walked inland and crossed the old road leading to the Money Pit. A short distance south of the old road, Nolan stopped and pointed to a slab of sandstone almost flush with the ground, saying, "There's the Head Stone." It looked like the bottom of a large dish, partly covered with topsoil and grass. The stone had been dug up, examined, photographed, and then laid back on its side with the face almost flush with the ground. "It's not in the exact position where we found it," Nolan said. "We didn't know what it meant at the time so we laid it aside a few feet. We were planning to dig a shaft here but we referenced its original position." Nolan pointed to an iron bar protruding a few inches out of the ground which he said "marks the original position of the stone."

The granite boulder at the end of the south arm of the Cross, lettered "B" on the plot plan, was about the same size and shape as the one at the shore; it had been tipped over but the indenture in the ground of its original position was clear. Nolan said they had discovered the remains of a wrought iron stove under the rock when they rolled it over and exposed its bottom. He also said they found small beach stones under the rock.

Continuing the tour of the Cross, Nolan showed me the cone-shaped stones on the stem. They were all of similar shape and size to the one at the beach. The two lower cones of the stem were undisturbed but the top one was misplaced by about 20 ft. It held no

Cone-shaped boulder on stem of Cross (Cone "D" on diagram).

significance to Nolan when it was disturbed, but fortunately the depression in the ground where it once rested was clearly visible and it was possible to estimate the original position of the top of the cone. A trail made by tractor treads and the dragging of a large heavy object led from the depression to the stone itself. Nolan said that the stone had been in the way of a line he was running and had told the machine operator to drag it out of the way. The stone had not been deliberately removed in relation to evidence regarding the Cross Nolan assured me.

"How many other boulders of similar size and shape might be found on the island?" I asked. Nolan replied that there were no others. He said that on surveying the entire island in 1961-62, he had not seen any granite boulders of the size and configuration that mark

91

off the Cross. During my tour of the Cross, I looked at about for boulders of a similar shape. I saw only one rock the size of the cones but it was far from being conical in shape. There were boulders on the shore of Joudrey's Cove, but a cursory search found nothing resembling the cones of the Cross.

Proceeding with my assignment, I estimated the original positions of the tops of the two cone-shaped boulders that were disturbed and carried out the survey. The arms of the Cross were found to be

Pit dubbed the "Treasure Site" by Nolan. A large mass of snugly packed granite boulders was removed from this excavation. (Pit partly filled with water.)

at right angles to the stem and all the measurements complied with Nolan's plot plan!

Two years later I was back on the island with Nolan but it wasn't to survey, verify measurements, or meet the press. He had made another astounding discovery associated with the Cross, and I was interested.

By running lines from drilled rocks in connection with the Cross Nolan had found what he referred to as the "Treasure Site." He had made the discovery at a place about 400 ft. east of the Cone "C" and 200 ft. more or less from the high water mark of Joudrey's Cove.

At his "Treasure Site" Nolan bit into the topsoil with his back-hoe and struck a stone barrier at a depth of 2 ft. He peeled away the

A pile of stones removed from the pit at Nolan's "Treasure Site."

An old tree stump from the bottom of the pit at Nolan's "Treasure Site."

topsoil and uncovered a paving of granite boulders covering an area about 40 ft. square. Each boulder weighed between 2 and 5 tons. Digging downward, he removed fifty-six boulders to a depth of 11 ft. "It was a compact mass of heavy granite boulders in a pit," he said. "They were definitely man-placed because the sides and bottom of the pit were in undisturbed soil but the soil inside the excavation between the boulders was loose. Nolan found large old tree stumps among the boulders at the bottom of the pit. "They didn't get down there under the rocks on their own," Nolan said. Further evidence that what Nolan had found was man-made came from the appearance of the stones. Nolan says that the boulders showed signs of "weathering on one side" proving that they were once above grade, probably collected off the beach at Joudrey's Cove.

That summer, Nolan barged a drilling rig over to the island and began exploring the ground beneath the excavation. The following summer, after a winter shut-down, the drilling work was resumed. Day after day, the drillers probed the depths below and then at about 11:00 A.M. on a summer morning, they struck what they believed was a void or cavity in the bedrock at a depth of 125 ft.!

Nolan has imposed a state of secrecy and has stayed tight-lipped about the operations to this day. "Drilling logs are being analyzed," Nolan says. "There may be a vault or cavern below; perhaps a tunnel entrance." That is all he will say about the excavation. But, he's elated and more optimistic than ever.

There is no doubt that Nolan is planning an extensive excavation in the near future. He recently remarked, "Numerous things that have been found in the swamp are currently under examination. Oak Island is so complex that there is no word to describe it. What I've learned would blow a computer!"

Although Nolan is convinced that success lies just around the corner, previous Oak Island treasure hunter, Isaac Blair, commented in a letter to his nephew Frederick L. Blair, a prominent person in the island's history: "I saw enough to convince me that there was treasure buried there and enough to convince me that they will never get it." I sincerely hope that he will someday be proven wrong!

CHAPTER EIGHT

HENRY SINCLAIR'S CASTLE

Alva Pye of New Ross, Nova Scotia, suspects that he may be sitting on a treasure of unfathomable value. In the backyard of his house, Pye's Seniors Boarding Home, lies what he and others contend is the remains of an ancient castle built by the Knights Templar—a medieval organization of immense wealth and power. Madness or rational? Two decades ago, the people of New Ross would have pronounced Alva Pye "certifiable" but not today! Visitors from two continents show up at all times of the day to see the "ruins." One visitor, a Scotsman, was so enthusiastic that, lacking transportation from the Halifax International Airport, he hitchhiked the nearly 80 mi. to see Pye's stone rubble.

All this excitement started after Pye and his wife bought the former home of Mrs. Joan Harris. There had been talk around the small community that Joan might perhaps be "a little touched" because she reportedly scraped and dug around the rocks in her backyard, and talked excitedly about uncovering the ruins of an ancient castle. But, in the late 1980s, the book *Holy Grail Across the Atlantic* by Michael Bradley hit the market. It touches on Joan Harris's struggle to persuade the scientific community to take her claim seriously, and theorizes that what she found was the ruins of a castle built in the late fourteenth century by Henry Sinclair, Earle of Orkney, of Scotland. Although the book disguises names and the place, calling Joan Harris "Jeanne McKay" and New Ross the "Cross" in an effort to prevent amateur investigation of the ruins and possible vandalism, few doubted that Jeanne was Joan Harris and the place was New Ross. The story caught fire and Joan's discovery took on an aura of credibility.

I FIRST LEARNED of Joan Harris's discovery in 1979 when I received a letter from her relating the following story: She and her husband bought a house in that community in 1972 that stands on a castle mound (the ruins of a castle). Nobody in the village was aware of the mound, but unlike she and her husband, they were not world travellers. "I am very familiar with castle mounds in Europe and of course the castles themselves," she explains, "and as soon as I saw our proposed new home I recognized it for what it was." Her attention to detail led her to "a path leading out and along the back, looping outwards to encircle two overgrown rocky mounds, just as I had seen such pathways going around the outside of castles in the U.K. and other countries." She had heard legends of such a place from Indians and from others who claimed seventeenth-century ancestors. The location was where they had told her "such a place had once existed." One family had until recently been in possession of old plans, now in the United States, dated seventeenth century. They made sketches for her and helped her trace the old walls. From them she learned that the castle had had seven towers but by the seventeenth century only the well tower and two others nearby at the back were standing. The others had been in ruins since the great front gateway arch collapsed, date unknown. Mrs. Harris went digging for information and says, "I later found pictures in a book of Norumbega Castle which fitted with the back part of our ruins and in fact our boundaries appear to be those of a later cut-off smaller castle which was built on the original site. We have unearthed old walls, the first set massive, the next 5 ft. wide and the latest (seventeenth century) only 3 ft. wide." Mrs. Harris went on to lay out her theories and discoveries:

> "My theory is that Sudhrike (the French called it *Souriquois*) was the mainland; the word means "Southern Kingdom" or "Domain in old Norse." Norumbega simply means "Northern Settlement," so it could have been attached first to an inland city and then, later, to northern lands in what is now New Brunswick. Everybody till now has looked for Norumbega City in Norumbega territory or somewhere else on the mainland.
>
> "Writings about Nerumbega City show that it was about

15 mi. inland; above the Bay of Many Islands. That fits this village in every respect, and the "Bay" could be Mahone Bay. There are signs of other buildings having been here and local people have told me that our house is built on an ancient cellar site.

"Could this be another Norse site, even Leif Erikson's inland capital? The Indians told me it was "The King's Refuge"; one finds "Refuge" on old maps, but the Nova Scotia peninsula is always omitted, giving the impression it was in New Brunswick.

"When we dug up part of a Viking sword, our theory seemed to be confirmed. We have also found a quantity of handmade nails at the foot of a strange looking block of stone which we have named "The Execution Block." They were in a small pit of blackened stones.

"Some of the rocks on our land and on the surrounding land have inscriptions on them. None mean anything in any modern language and I have checked that they are not Norse ruins. The only letter plainly decipherable is an "N" with a line running under it across the rock but not pointing north. The rock could have been moved slightly, though it is too large for two men to move, as we tried. Some people think this is a surveyor's mark. However, I have since then discovered that Ogam has lines such as this one, and as there are other letters or characters on the rock which are too weathered to read properly, it may have been Ogam rather than a Roman "N." I believe that in Ogam "N" meant "H."

"The so-called execution block was lying on its back and we used to call it "the headless statue" because of its shape (head and shoulders protruding at an angle from the earth). On the head is a deeply carved cross, not the Christian kind but an "X." When we at length dug this rock out it turned out to be a Celtic herm, which put a different slant on everything.

"Another quite deeply carved rock is indecipherable. It too has a line running across it, with a perfect semicircle deeply carved at one end and what looks like an eye, badly weathered, at the other.

"We next identified a pagan fertility stone, of the same shape as many which I have seen in the U.K. These date from prehistoric times, e.g. 800 B.C.

"Ranging further out, I examined other stones already

recognized by us as building stones of some sort. One of them was carved in lettering which I by this time could identify as probably Punic. There are as you know theories that old civilizations which disappeared from Europe, etc., ended up here, the remnants fleeing across the Atlantic. Some of the huge blocks lying around reminded me of Stonehenge. There are not many now, but coupled with one or two Punic inscriptions and a Celtic herm, fertility stone, etc., they could indicate an old stone circle. The location of these stones is an extensive flattened hilltop adjacent to this castle site. One of the large blocks has a "star map" on it—each star represented by a cupule. I had some difficulty at first in deciphering it, but this was because the Great Bear seemed to be upside down. I consulted my encyclopaedia and discovered that the Great Bear has varied through the ages. I assume that one could date the site from this inverted Great Bear.

"While I was investigating what is here, I naturally took in such mysteries as the Ovens (old abandoned gold mine on the South Shore of Nova Scotia near the town of Lunenburg) and Oak Island. The river here (near Oak Island) is the Gold River. Leif Erikson returned home a wealthy man. Was it gold he discovered rather than grapes? The term Ovens is an old one meaning smelters: the site was called that long before the mini gold rush of the 1880s. The gold then found was along the shore. Was it from the tailings of ancient smelters?

"I have passed on details of what we have discovered here to various people in the hope of getting the site "authenticated." All complain that it is not an authenticated site and to be honest I do not know to whom one must go to get this done. I have tried everybody on this continent from the Nova Scotia Museum (they say they are not interested if it is before about 1800, 1700 at earliest) to various universities both here and in the United States. Some from the U.S. have photographed things here, but then we heard no more. One university told me that there was nothing to prove I had not faked all the rocks and moved them around. Many weigh several hundred-weights, if not tons!"

Mrs. Harris ended her letter with an invitation to "come and see this new Nova Scotia mystery." I was particularly busy on engineering and surveying projects and procrastinated. Time and again I would make plans to drive to New Ross, only to break them for one emergency or another. When I finally found the time to visit, Mrs. Harris and her husband had moved. But this fragment of history is still being pursued.

In 1992, while writing a book about Oak Island, I received calls from a group of people who were investigating the validity of suggested theories outlined in several revolutionary books about the Knights Templar Order. The theories, which suggested a very different view of the discovery and exploration of Canada, tied in with the New Ross castle and its discovery—a Knights Templar connection.

The books in question are Michael Bradley's *Holy Grail Across the Atlantic*, and *The Holy Blood and the Holy Grail* by Michael Baigent, Richard Leigh, and Henry Lincoln. According to these books, the Knights Templar was founded in 1118 A.D. under the name of the Order of the Poor Knights of Christ and the Temple of Solomon, nineteen years after the capture of the Holy City during the First Christian Crusade. It was a shadowy order of warrior-monks who played a crucial role in the Christian Crusades and fought and died by the thousands. These monks, dressed in white capes with splayed red crosses were the storm troopers in the siege of the Holy Land. They fought to reclaim the sepulchre of Jesus Christ and the Holy Land from the Muslim infidels.

The Templars were pledged to obedience, poverty, and chastity and owed allegiance only to the Pope. They were consequently totally independent of the rule of any king, prince or prelate. Admission to the order required the signing over of all possessions by the new recruit. The Templar's holdings proliferated as the sons of noble families throughout Europe swelled the order, and as vast amounts of money, goods, and land were donated by wealthy Crusade supporters. Although all the donations and gifts were accepted, the order disposed of nothing. It was forbidden by its constitution to part with anything—not even to ransom a leader.

The Templars created the system of modern banking and became the bankers for every throne in Europe by lending large sums to destitute monarchs. They possessed their own seaports, shipyards, and fleet. As well as amassing great wealth, the Templars became a powerful organization with strong international influences and often acted as mediators between nobles and monarchs throughout all the Western world and the Holy Land. But their wealth, influence, and independence were short-lived.

By 1306 the Crusades were over, the Holy Land was almost

entirely under Muslim control, and the Templars had lost their *raison d'être*. King Philippe IV of France was determined to rid his country of the order. They had a military force much stronger than his, they were arrogant and unruly, they were firmly established throughout his country and, most importantly, he owed them a lot of money. Philippe gained the Pope's support and compiled a list of charges which were in part taken from information provided by his spies who had infiltrated the order. With sufficient accusations to deliver his blow, he issued secret orders to his agents throughout the country which stipulated a simultaneous arrest of all Templars in France at dawn on Friday, October 13, 1307; and all their estates and goods were to be confiscated for the Crown. Although a number of knights escaped the dragnet, the arrest was successful, but Philippe's main objective—acquisition of the Templar's immense wealth—failed. The treasure of the Templars had mysteriously disappeared.

According to rumour, the order had received advance warning of the planned arrest and the treasure was smuggled by night from its Paris estates and transported by wagons to the coast and the Templar's naval base at LaRochelle. There, the fortune was loaded onto eighteen galleys and shipped off to sea—never to be heard of again. Although the Pope officially dissolved the Knights Templar in 1312 under pressure by the King, the order wasn't completely wiped out. A number of knights escaped, remained at large, or were acquitted of wrongdoing and the Order went underground. Philippe tried to persuade his fellow monarchs of other European countries to co-operate in eliminating the order, but he was not wholly successful. A number of Templars were arrested in England but most received only light sentences such as a few years of penance in an abbey or monastery.

Many knights found refuge in Scotland which was at war with England at the time. According to legend, the order maintained itself as a coherent body in Scotland for another four hundred years and a substantial contingent of the Templars is said to have fought on the side of Robert Bruce in the 1314 Battle of Bennockburn. In Lorraine, which at the time was part of Germany, the order was supported by the duke of the principality, and in Portugal the order simply modified its name to "Knights of Christ" and continued on well into the 1500s.

A CONNECTION BETWEEN Joan Harris's castle mound and the Templars may seem tenuous, but the folks who phoned me were adamant. They professed that Henry Sinclair, who they believe was a

Templar, visited Nova Scotia near the turn of the fourteenth century either to conceal or to recover the treasure of the Templars. After several months of exploring, he built a refuge castle at New Ross. He chose this location because it lies near the centre of the narrowest part of the Nova Scotia peninsula and could be found either by following the Gold River up from the Atlantic or the Gaspereau River from the Bay of Fundy.

My callers also speculated that the castle could have been built hundreds of years before Sinclair's visit. According to this version of the tale, Sinclair knew of the whereabouts of the refuge. When he arrived he found the castle in ruins but proceeded to build a new one on its foundation.

I found the castle speculations slightly more credible after a bit of Saint-Clair research. The Templars who fled to Scotland found refuge among the Saint-Clairs of Rosslyn, Midlothian. Henry Sinclair (also spelled St. Clair) was born to the Lord of Rosslyn, only a generation after the Templar dispersal. Henri de Saint-Clair, Henry Sinclair's ancestor and namesake fought alongside of Godfroi de Bouillion (credited with capturing the Holy City in 1099) during the siege of Jerusalem and several Saint-Clairs became Templars.

Henry Sinclair was born at Rosslyn Castle near Edinburg, Scotland, in 1345. He became a knight at the age of twenty-one and was the Grand Master of the Scottish Masons. At that time, he was elevated to Earle of Orkney and Lord of Shetland. Although the Orkland and Shetland islands were owned by Norway, Henry was born heir to these northern territories by a complicated line of feudal inter-marriages.

Although owned by Norway, the Orkney and Shetland Islands had been independent for some years. Henry's earldom required a navy to control it, for its most valuable natural resource was a fishing industry.

Henry Sinclair was successful in building a substantial fleet to meet the needs of his earldom but he worried about the absence of gunpower on his ships. Cannon on board a ship was a new technology that had been recently implemented by Carlo Zeno, "The Lion" of Venice, at the Battle of Chioggia against the Genoese.

The brothers of Carlo Zeno, Nicola and Antonia, joined Henry Sinclair in Scotland and provided the necessary expertise on forging lightweight cannon for shipboard use. In addition to their skills at weaponry, they also possessed the latest skills in navigation and cartography.

Nicolo and Antonio corresponded regularly with their brother Carlo in Venice. This correspondence became known to historians as the "Zeno Narrative." According to the Zeno Narrative, as far back as 1371, four fishing boats owned by Sinclair subjects were blown out to sea and came ashore on a distant land far to the west (probably Newfoundland). After spending twenty years there and on lands to the south, one of them was picked up by European fishermen and returned to Scotland. Sinclair resolved to explore these lands, and set sail with a fleet of twelve vessels resembling Viking ships.

The Zeno Narrative, by Antonio Zeno, tells of Henry Sinclair's expedition:

"The nobleman [Sinclair] is therefore resolved to send forth a fleet toward those parts, and there are so many who desire to join in the expedition on account of the novelty and strangeness of the thing that I think we shall be very strongly appointed without any public expense at all.

"I set sail with a considerable number of vessels and men, but had not the chief command, as I had expected to have, for Sinclair went in his own person.

"Our great preparations for the voyage to Estotiland were in an unlucky hour; for exactly three days before our departure, the fisherman died who was to have been our guide: nevertheless, Zichmni (Sinclair) would not give up the enterprise, but in lieu of the deceased fisherman, took some sailors who had come out with him from the island.

"Steering westward, we sighted some islands subject to Frislanda, and passing certain shoals, came to Ledovo, where we stayed seven days to refresh ourselves and furnish the fleet with necessities. Departing thence, we arrived on the first of April at the island of Ilofe; and as the wind was full in our favour, pushed on. But not long thereafter, when on the open ocean, there arose so great a storm that for eight days we were continuously in toil, and driven we knew not where, and a considerable number of vessels were lost to each other. At length, when the storm abated, we gathered together the scattered vessels, and sailing with a prosperous wind, we sighted land on the west.

"Steering straight for it, we reached a quiet and safe harbour, in which we saw a very large number of armed people, who came running, prepared to defend the island.

Sinclair now caused his men to make signs of peace to them, and they sent ten men to us who could speak ten languages, but we could understand none of them, except one who was from Iceland.

"Being brought before our Prince and asked what was the name of the island, and what people inhabited it, and who was governor, he answered that the island was called Icaria, and that all the kings there were called Icari, after the first king, who was the son of Daedalus, King of Scotland.

"Daedalus conquered the island, left his son there for king, and gave them those laws that they retain to the present time. After that, when going to sail further, he was drowned in a great tempest; and in memory of his death that sea was called to this day the Icarian Sea, and the kings of this island were called Icari. They were content with the state which God had given them, and would neither alter their laws nor admit any stranger.

"They therefore requested our Prince not to attempt to interfere with their laws, which they received from that king of worthy memory, and observed up to the present time; that the attempt would lead to his own destruction, for they were all prepared to die rather than relax in any way the use of those laws. Nevertheless, that we might not think that they altogether refused intercourse with other men, they ended by saying that they would willingly receive one of our people, and give him an honorable position among them, if only for the sake of learning our language and gaining information as to our customs, in the same way as they had already received those ten other persons from ten different countries, who had come into their island.

"To all this our Prince made no reply, beyond inquiring where there was a good harbour, and making signs that he intended to depart.

"Accordingly, sailing around about the island, he put in with all his fleet in full sail, into a harbour which he found on the eastern side. The sailors went ashore to take in wood and water, which they did as quickly as they could, for fear that they might be attacked by the islanders and not without reason, for the inhabitants made signals to their neighbours by fire and smoke, and taking their arms, the others coming to their aid, they all came running down to the seaside upon our men with bows and arrows, so that many were slain and several wounded. Although we made signs of peace to them, it was of no use, for their rage increased more and more, as though they were fighting for their own existence.

"Being compelled to depart, we sailed along in a great circuit about the island, being always followed on the hilltops and along the seacoasts by a great number of armed men. At length, doubling the north cape of the island, we came upon many shoals, amongst which we were for ten days in continuous danger of losing our fleet, but fortunately all that time the weather was very fine. All the way till we came to the east cape we saw the inhabitants still on hilltops and by the sea coast, howling and shooting at us from a distance to show their animosity towards us.

"We therefore resolved to put into some safe harbour, and see if we might once again speak with the Icelander; but we failed in our object; for the people more like beasts than men, stood constantly prepared to beat us back if we should attempt to come on land. Wherefore, Sinclair, seeing that he could do nothing, and if he were to persevere in this attempt, the fleet would fall short of provisions, took his departure with a fair wind and sailed six days to the westwards; but the winds shifting to the southwest, and the sea becoming rough, we sailed four days with the wind aft, and finally sighted land.

"As the sea ran high and we did not know what country it was, we were afraid at first to approach it, but by God's blessing the wind lulled, and then there came on a great calm. Some of the crew pulled ashore and soon returned with great joy with news that they found an excellent country and a still better harbour. We brought our barks and our boats to land, and on entering an excellent harbour, we saw in the distance a great hill that poured forth smoke, which gave us hope that we should find some inhabitants in the island. Neither would Sinclair rest, though it was a great way off, without sending one hundred soldiers to explore the country, and bring us an account of what sort of people the inhabitants were.

"Meanwhile, we took in a store of wood and water, and caught a considerable quantity of fish and sea fowl. We also found such an abundance of bird's eggs that our men, who were half famished, ate of them to repletion.

"While we were at anchor there, the month of June came

in, and the air in the island was mild and pleasant beyond description; but as we saw nobody, we began to suspect that this pleasant place was uninhabited. To the harbour we gave the name of Trin, and the headland which stretched out into the sea was called Cape Trin.

"After eight days the one hundred soldiers returned, and brought word that they had been through the island and up to the hill, and that the smoke was a natural thing proceeding from a great fire in the bottom of the hill, and that there was a spring from which issued a certain substance like pitch, which ran into the sea, and that thereabouts dwelt a great many people half wild, and living in caves. They were of small stature and very timid. They reported also there was a large river, and a very good and safe harbour.

"When Sinclair heard this, and noticed the wholesome and pure atmosphere, fertile soil, good rivers, and so many other conveniences, he conceived the idea of founding a settlement. But his people, fatigued, began to murmur, and say they wished to return to their homes for winter was not far off, and if they allowed it once to set in, they would not be able to get away before the following summer. He therefore retained only boats propelled by oars, and such of his people as were willing to stay, and sent the rest away in ships, appointing me, against my will, to be their captain.

"Having no choice, therefore, I departed and sailed twenty days to the eastwards without sight of any land; then, turning my course towards the southeast, in five days I sighted on land, and found myself on the island of Neome and knowing the country, I perceived I was past Iceland; and as the inhabitants were subject to Sinclair, I took in fresh stores and sailed in three days to Frislanda, where the people, who thought they had lost their Prince, in consequence of his long absence on the voyage we had made, received us with a heavy welcome.... Concerning those things that you desire to know of me, as to the people and their habits, the animals, and the countries adjoining, I have written about it all in a separate book, which please God, I shall bring with me. In it I have described the country, the monstrous fishes, the customs and laws of Frislanda, of Iceland, of Shetland, the Kingdom of Norway, Estotiland and Drogio; and lastly, I have written ... the life and exploits of Sinclair, a Prince as worthy of immortal memory as any that ever lived, for his great bravery and remarkable goodness."

Although the Zeno Narrative gives no date of voyage, the American historian and author, Frederick Pohl, found a way of dating the expedition. Noting that it was common for explorers to name their discoveries from the religious calendar, Pohl seized on the statements "while we were at anchor there, the month of June came in" and "To the harbour we gave the name Trin." Might "Trin" refer to Trinity Sunday which is the eighth Sunday following Easter? Historical records indicate that Henry Sinclair died in August 1400 so his voyage was earlier. Pohl searched the dates of past Easter celebrations and selected June 2, 1398, from the following Trinity Sundays: June 6, 1395; June 28, 1396; June 17, 1397; June 2, 1398; May 25, 1399; June 13, 1400.

Pohl figured that June 2, 1398, was the most likely date because it is the closest day to "the month of June came in." For my own part, I can't be sure. Pohl may have thought that two years was long enough to be away from home but I think it is relevant that Antonio says on returning to Frislanda (the Orkney Islands of Scotland), "the people, who thought they had lost their Prince, in consequence of his long absence on the voyage." Would two years have been considered a "long absence"? Could the date have been June 6, 1395? The month of June might have been considered to have "came in" while at anchor on the first week, and Trinity Sunday would have still been an appropriate day from which to take a name. However, Pohl's method of deduction is clever and most historians accept June 2, 1398. But my comment should be taken seriously by those who feel that Sinclair may have needed more time than two years to accomplish all for which he is credited.

Nova Scotia is thought to be the second "island" of Henry Sinclair's expedition because of the Zeno Narrative statements, "we saw in the distance a great hill that poured forth smoke" and "the smoke was a natural thing proceeding from a great fire in the bottom of the hill, and that there was a spring from which issued a certain substance like pitch, which ran into the sea, and that thereabouts dwelt a great many people half wild, and living in caves." In 1951, Dr. William H. Hobbs, a University of Michigan geologist, pointed out that the only pitch deposits in the coastal region of North America were at Stellarton and Pictou in Nova Scotia.

Pitch deposits of Stellarton do indeed run into the tidal river.

The Stellarton pitch deposits have in the past burned out of control. And, it was only in the Stellarton region that the Mi'kmaq lived in caves.

Presuming that the "great hill that poured forth smoke" is Mount Adams, Pohl drew a straight line from the Stellarton pitch deposits through the mountain to the Atlantic Ocean. His line struck Chedabucto Bay and he concluded that the harbour "Trin" where Henry Sinclair landed was most likely Guysborough Harbour at the head of the bay.

The Zeno Narrative tells nothing of Henry Sinclair's activities after landing in Nova Scotia. Antonia Zeno writes only of his own return to Frislanda. However, the narrative indicates that Sinclair was interested in exploring the country and making contact with its inhabitants. He sent one hundred of his men to investigate the "great hill that poured forth smoke," to explore the country and find out "what sort of people the inhabitants were." His men returned with word of people living in caves and a "very good and safe harbour." Believing the land he had found was an island, it seems reasonable that he followed the shore around to the Stellarton area where he ingratiated himself to the Indians and used their help to explore the new country.

All might be guesswork except for Frederick Pohl. He constructed Sinclair's comings and goings from Mi'kmaq legends about the man-god, Glooscap. Pohl identified Glooscap as Henry Sinclair from a long list of specific similarities, one being that they both had three daughters. Other scholars had accepted Glooscap as being a European, so Pohl's identification came as no great surprise.

In his book, *Prince Henry Sinclair*, Pohl attempts to trace Glooscap's movements. Mi'kmaq legends say that before the onset of winter, Glooscap made a return trip across the Nova Scotia peninsula from the Bay of Fundy to the Atlantic. Pohl surmises that Glooscap (Henry Sinclair) paddled west along the Bay of Fundy shore of Nova Scotia to the Annapolis Basin and the present site of Digby. From Digby, he paddled east to Annapolis Royal. From Annapolis he reached the Atlantic via the lake system that crosses the peninsula to the Mersey River, which empties into the ocean at Liverpool. This is a logical route for it provides an almost uninterrupted waterway. One of the lakes in the system is Lake Rossignol, the largest lake on the Nova Scotia peninsula. Following the cross-country exploration, Sinclair wintered on Cape d'Or on the Bay of Fundy. Michael Bradley, in his book *Holy Grail Across the Atlantic*, suggests that Pohl is wrong in supposing that Sinclair returned by the same route. He writes, "Surely, any explorer would want to see as much of the country as possible, and would therefore use two different routes, to cross to the Atlantic and to return to Fundy." Bradley believes that since the Annapolis to Liverpool route crosses the widest part of the Nova Scotia peninsula, Sinclair would have wanted to get an idea of the general width of the peninsula by crossing it at its narrowest. He therefore takes the liberty of revising Pohl's map of Sinclair's journeys to show the shorter return crossing by the Gold and Gaspereau Rivers. By this revision, Bradley supports the case for Henry Sinclair's visit to New Ross and the castle.

Antonio Zeno writes in the narrative that Henry Sinclair conceived the idea of founding a settlement after he landed in Nova Scotia and took stock of the "wholesome and pure atmosphere, fertile soil, good rivers, and so many other conveniences." However, one is led to believe that this idea was quashed by some of his people who were anxious to return home before the winter began to set in. But, Michael Bradley suggests that Sinclair may have, indeed, carried out his idea. And, if he had, the best place for the settlement would have been in the middle of the peninsula, where Joan Harris claimed to have found castle ruins.

Scientists have searched for evidence of a colonial settlement at Cape d'Or where Sinclair, according to legend, spent the winter. They found nothing that would provide definitive proof of a settlement.

Bradley points out that Cape d'Or would not have been a good choice for a settlement. It is a rocky promontory with insufficient land for farming. And, it would never have served as a good place for a refuge as it is "too obvious a landmark and landfall for anyone sailing up the Bay of Fundy either by accident or design." Bradley suggests that Joan Harris's castle site would have made an ideal refuge. Situated as it is on a hilltop in the centre of the peninsula, it would have provided a lookout to either side.

Bradley suggests that a settlement or refuge could have been established without the Indians knowledge. He thinks that Sinclair could have divided his force, leaving some at Cape d'Or while taking the rest to New Ross. He says that the Indians would not necessarily have known what was going on as they were relatively immobile in the winter because the water routes were closed to them by ice. As long as Sinclair was at Cape d'Or before winter set in and there in the spring, the Indians would have assumed that he had spent the winter there.

Indeed, the Mi'kmaq legends say nothing specific about Glooscap's winter activities. It may be gathered that they thought Glooscap spent the winter at Cape d'Or. And, they may have been mistaken. The Indians used the canoe as a principle means of transportation. As neither the Gold River nor the Gaspereau River is navigable for any appreciable distance, Bradley contends that few Mi'kmaq could have inhabited New Ross in Sinclair's day.

Whether establishing a settlement or refuge or staying put at Cape d'Or, Sinclair and his men apparently spent a busy winter, for in the spring Sinclair unveiled what the Mi'kmaq called a "stone canoe." It is believed that the Indians referred to the boat in this way because men walked on its deck as if it were an island and the masts and sails looked like trees. After he had launched his boat, Glooscap threw a farewell banquet to which all were invited and then sailed away.

Frederick Pohl speculates that Sinclair sailed to the New England coast and marched inland to the summit of a high hill, now called Prospect Hill. From this hill, at an altitude of 465 ft., he viewed his newly discovered land from all directions.

Pohl's speculation is supported by an effigy of a fourteenth-century knight punched into a ledge of the hill. It is known as "The Westford Knight." Apparently, one of Sinclair's men lost his life in the climb to the top. The figure outlined by the weather-worn punch holes carries the symbol of death, a broken sword.

I DROPPED IN on Alva Pye one sunny afternoon in August, uninvited and unexpected. Although I was interrupting the work of a busy day, Alva seemed unperturbed. He slipped into the house and returned with a thick file folder. "I made a package of some of this stuff that I collected, and I was giving these to people," he explained, "and when you start giving things away, they don't go very far. Plus you run out of money."

Alva opened the file and withdrew a floor plan sketch of a castle. With no explanation as to its origin, Alva quickly pointed out the main features on the ground that matched those on his sketch. "There is your well tower," he said, pointing to a 3 ft. high stone that protruded upward from a base of smaller rocks. "This is where the walls of the castle start and it is also the holy well and over to your left and right, those two big rocks mark two of the towers," Alva said, pointing towards the rear of his property, while referring to his sketch. "Those rocks weren't pushed there by a bulldozer or other kind of machine," Alva explained, "because if they were, you would be able to tell … hauling marks and so on." Alva pointed out that a portion of the castle wall is missing. He said, "There used to be a wall from that tree down that way but, of course, when people cultivated this land and grubbed it off, they got rid of some of the wall."

"You can't see the walls as they originally were," Alva explained. "Stone walls don't stay up long around here and also they didn't make very good concrete in those days. It just turned to sand. For example, there was a stone wall on our property when I was a kid. Rock was put there every time we cultivated the land. We'd drag the stones over and place them on the wall. I was about sixteen years old when

Small excavation on outside edge of rock wall of the "Sinclair Castle." Most of the stones of the "Castle" foundation are obscured by grass.

I last worked there and the wall was about this high." Alva held up his hand, indicating a height of about 6 or 7 ft. "Then, a little while ago I took my young fellow fishing and we walked by the wall and I stepped on it. It was only a couple of feet high. It had countersunk that quick. I'm forty-eight now, so that would have only been thirty-two years ago."

Returning my attention to the holy well, Alva reminisced, "When I was ten or eleven years old, we went to Sunday School in a big house on Mill Road, up the other end of New Ross from here. It had a big living room and that's where we'd have our classes and one of the ladies that lived there was our teacher. So, the subject one day had something to do with holy water because when I left the class to come out to get a drink of water I asked the old gentleman who was sitting there who was ninety some years old.... I said, is this water holy? Sort of joking, right? Cause we were just talking about it in our class. He said 'no, but if you're really interested in holy water, they claim there was a well in the New Ross area that had holy water and the Indians used to say it was healing water.' The old man said healing or holy or something to that nature and that was the last time I heard anything about it until my aunt was visiting one day. She has taken a great interest in this place in the last little while because

The "Well Tower." The rock marks the location of the holy well.

apparently that rock there (referring to the stone marking the holy well) had a figure or a face on it and you could see it at night when you turned your car lights on it. It was on this day that my aunt said, 'I can remember my grandmother talking about a well that had healing water in it.' Then my aunt asked me, 'I wonder if that's what that was' (referring to the holy well.). Then, one day my wife said, 'Didn't the McKay's say that there was a well on this property that contained healing water?' "

I asked Alva if he was referring to the Harris couple when he used the name McKay and if so why. He explained that he had not yet read Bradley's book when his wife referred to the McKays and the "holy well" and the name McKay stuck. Also, he has got into the habit of using the name McKay in place of Harris as he has trouble relating Joan Harris to Jeanne McKay. He said, "When I was growing up in New Ross, we always assumed that the Harrises were a little batty, both oars not in the water, so to speak." The name McKay has a more credible feel to Alva than Harris. Alva said, "I now think that it was us who were off the beaten path—the backward ones—not the Harrises."

Alva says that he and a gentleman from a university in Vancouver temporarily removed some of the rocks from the alleged "holy well" and verified that it is, indeed, a well. He is adamant that the "holy well" was never dug by anyone in New Ross and "it didn't grow

The Masonic Lodge is approximately across the highway from the Pye home. Some Henry Sinclair researchers have suggested that the proximity may not be coincidental.

there." Alva pointed out some strange marks and figures etched on one side of the upright stone of the "holy well." He doesn't profess to be able to decipher the etchings and believes that they may be written in a language that we don't understand. Inside the alleged castle walls, Alva pointed out what he says is the foundation of the "castle." It is a discernible 10 by 12 ft. rectangular outline of stones which show no appearance of having been recently placed.

Alva defends the small size which to most people seems ridiculously tiny for a "castle." He says, "Lionel Fanthorpe of the BBC and world authority on unsolved mysteries took a look at the "castle" and he said that it is the precise size that the castle would have been because only one person would have stayed there." But not everyone agrees.

Michael Bradley visited the Harrises a few times during 1982 and 1983 and studied the alleged castle site. He contends that what appears to be a building foundation in the Harris backyard is only one small segment of the total castle; that this tiny building was too small for human habitation but given its proximity to the "holy well" might have housed anything from a forge to a bakery; most of the castle was off the Harris property, snaking out over adjacent lands.

However, Pye is not put off by Bradley's opinion and accepts the small building as an authentic castle. Armed with Joan Harris's theories and discoveries and the stones that dominate his backyard, Alva Pye is about to go commercial. For now, he doesn't plan to try and uncover a Templar treasure but has a more pragmatic project in mind. He will rebuild the castle!

Alva plans to uncover what is left of his castle walls, reconstruct it to a predetermined height and charge admission. He says, "So, I think if I can get the proper people to do it and clean everything right off, the sod, the weed, the bush, everything right down to the earth, build the rock castle, build the walls around, in other words, recon-struct it, I'll have accomplished something. But it doesn't have to be 20 ft. high, just enough so they can walk in and say, 'Yeah! I can see what you're talking about.' "

Alva doesn't place any emphasis on an immediate financial return. He says, "I'll have a gate or whatever and have it fenced off and maybe I can get enough off of it on admissions to pay for having it done."

Alva is not opposed to having someone join his venture. But there would be stipulations. The backer or partner must share his interest in recreating the castle, and his determination to "never be controlled by the government."

CHAPTER NINE

ANOTHER OAK ISLAND

I had passed the signpost many times. It read "Oak Island Road." But it wasn't in the Mahone Bay area or anywhere nearby. The sign referred to another Oak Island situated in the Minas Basin of the Bay of Fundy, on the opposite side of the Nova Scotia peninsula 35 mi. from the Mahone Bay island.

Two islands with the same name seemed insignificant in a province where duplication of place names is common. In Nova Scotia villages islands, rivers, brooks, and lakes quite commonly share the same name. There is a community named Brookfield in the central part of the province and a North and South Brookfield in the west. There are at least eight Salmon Rivers, many Trout Brooks, four or more Lewis Lakes, and many "Long" and "Round" islands, and the list goes on. So, the existence of another Oak Island[1] presented no enigma. At least not until a few years ago.

The inquisitive folks who phoned me in 1992 and talked about the alleged Henry Sinclair castle at New Ross had much more to tell. They speculated that there is a connection between the two Oak Islands. And, yes, believe it or not, the Fundy Oak Island may have its own "Money Pit."

Coincidentally, the two Oak Islands share a number of characteristics. Neither Oak Island is a true "island" by definition, although both were "real" islands at an earlier time. The Oak Island of Mahone Bay ceased to be an island in 1965 when Robert Dunfield, a

California petroleum geologist, built a one-lane causeway across the straight separating the west end of the island from the mainland. The causeway which is in use today was constructed by Dunfield to transport heavy excavation equipment to the Money Pit. The Fundy "Oak Island" became connected to the mainland as a result of extensive dykes built to reclaim large areas of fertile farmlands from the sea.

Beautiful groves of oaks once shrouded the camel-back hills of the Mahone Bay island. (Few if any of these oaks remain today due to disease and insect infestation, but a new growth is beginning to take up residency among the present-day evergreens.) The Fundy island supports a magnificent grove of oaks that reflects a mirror image of the grove that once adorned the Money Pit and its environs.

Both Oak Islands are near the mouth of a river. The Mahone Bay island is about 2 mi. south of where the Gold River spills into the sea. The Bay of Fundy island is about the same distance north of where the Gaspereau River empties into the Bay of Fundy.

The similarities were brought to my attention by the inquisitive investigators who speculated about the Castle. They believe that the resemblance is meaningful and that the Mahone and Fundy Oak Islands served a dual function. They marked the location of two routes to the "castle."

The investigators pointed out that the New Ross Castle is situated in the watershed area of both the Gold and Gaspereau Rivers which empty into the sea on opposite sides of the Nova Scotia peninsula. The watershed area is about halfway between the outlets of the two rivers, both of which are conveniently near the narrowest part of the Nova Scotia peninsula. The castle architect took advantage of this fact and situated his site where it could be accessed by water from either side of the province by the shortest available route.

The investigators say that an oak treed island situated near the mouths of both rivers is no coincidence. They were the only ones in either bay that supported a grove of oaks. Being unique in appearance, they served as beacons or signposts for the ancient mariners seeking the New Ross Castle. Once they located these islands, the rest was easy. Stand on either Oak Island and face the mainland and the mouth of a river is close by on your right. Follow that river to its end and you find yourself at the castle.

But why two routes? The investigators had done their homework. They explained that the early mariners experienced considerable difficulty finding their way around.

Latitude, the position north or south of the equator, was

determined in the northern hemisphere by measuring the altitude of Polaris (also known as the North or Pole Star) above the horizon in degrees. However, obtaining this angle from a small ship pitching around in a rough sea was difficult, and even experienced yachtsmen today using modern sextants have some difficulty. The medieval sailor had no sextant as it had not yet been developed. He estimated the angle above the horizon with the number of "hands" and "fingers" that would fill the height, or obtained a little more accuracy with a crude instrument called a "backstaff," which is an ancestor of the modern sextant.

Errors in angular measurements in the order of 3° were common, and since 1° of latitude is approximately equal to 70 mi., a captain could be more than 200 mi. north or south of the point he was seeking and be none the wiser. Furthermore, areas of the North Atlantic are frequently fog-bound or clouded over for hours and even days. After spending what may have seemed an eternity in a fogbank, when the clouds separated and stars became visible, the captain might have found that he had drifted miles off course.

But, if estimating or measuring latitude was difficult and sometimes inaccurate, determining longitude (position east or west of a given place) was formidably difficult and often carried out with only the wildest of guesses; indeed, the medieval mariner could not calculate his longitude with any measure of certainty. Longitude at sea could not be accurately determined until the chronometer (an instrument for measuring time precisely) was invented in the eighteenth century. Therefore, the mariner relied on his experience to estimate his position of longitude. With past knowledge of the time it took to sail between points of known distance under variable conditions of wind and current, he estimated and logged his daily progress.

When the medieval mariner set sail for Nova Scotia, all he probably could have done when leaving Europe was for the most part determine a course, log his estimated mileage and, visibility permitting, check the night sky to see if he was maintaining the correct latitude.

If a mariner had chosen a latitude of say 44$^{1/2}$°, and his measurements proved accurate, he might have stayed within a quarter of a degree of that line. If by chance he arrived dead on target, he would have entered Halifax Harbour. One-quarter degree to the north of his chosen latitude would have landed him near Ship Harbour, about 40 mi. up the coast from Halifax Harbour. One-quarter degree to the south would have landed him in Mahone Bay or St. Margaret's Bay, the harbour immediately to the east of Mahone Bay.

In view of the magnitude of latitude errors that sailors of old committed, what were the chances of ever finding the Gold River? Lengthwise, the province lies on a northeast to southwest line. A mariner would only have to make an error of 80 mi. off the true latitude of Mahone Bay to slip by the southern tip of the province and end up in the Bay of Fundy.

This is precisely where the Fundy Oak Island served its purpose. When a mariner missed his harbour or island, he conducted a search known as "latitude sailing." It consisted of sailing north or south to the latitude of the place he sought, and then sailing east or west until he found his destination. If he failed, the exercise was repeated, sometimes over and over again, perhaps reaching out further and further to the east or west while varying the latitude of the search.

Finding himself in the waters of the Bay of Fundy, the castle searcher would conduct the usual "latitude sailing" exercise and eventually come upon the oak-treed island in the Minas Basin.

One might ask why in either bay there was only one island with oaks growing on it. The investigators had the answer to this question. Henry Sinclair, or the Templars who may have preceded him, planted the trees. Otherwise, two bays, each having only one oak-treed island would have had to be a fluke of nature, and the odds against such an occurrence were remote.

As further proof that the two Oak Islands are unique, the investigators pointed out that the islands were noted by mariners as having oak forests, and people who settled these shores named them accordingly.

The peanut-shaped Mahone Oak Island is about 3/4 mi. long by 1,000 ft. wide at its narrowest section near the centre. The long portion runs in an east to west direction and its west end is separated from the mainland by a strait of water only about 600 ft. wide. This island appears as a peninsula or point of the mainland when approached from out in the bay. You have to sail close to the mainland to ascertain that it was really an island before being connected by a causeway.

As the Oak Islands allegedly served as beacons or signposts, the mariner entering either bay looked for an island of oaks that would direct him to the river leading to the castle. But wouldn't the island have to "stand out" from the landscape of the shore to be detected? What if the mainland had been similarly populated with oaks? Would the island have "stood out" against a non-contrasting backdrop?

The investigators argue that obviousness was not necessarily a factor. Certainly the mainland may have featured similar vegetation—not necessarily all oaks but stands of mixed hardwood—oak, maple, birch, etc. The islands of oaks need only to have had significance for a mariner who knew what he was looking for.

THE INVESTIGATORS who talked with me concerning the New Ross Castle believe that the treasure being sought on the Mahone Oak Island may actually be buried beneath the oaks of the second island. They point out that for over two hundred years people have been excavating the Money Pit on the Mahone Oak Island, tearing up the reconstructed beach, trying to find where the water comes from and, generally, making a mess by excavating holes all over the eastern end of the island. But they still haven't solved the riddle of the Money Pit. They excavate. They reach a depth of 100 ft., water floods in, and they dig again.

Two centuries of digging and the application of modern technology—drilling, heavy excavation equipment, construction of cofferdams, television cameras, you name it—have brought up nothing in the way of a treasure, only tantalizing bits (a piece of parchment, small sections of a gold chain) that continue to spur them on. But, what if the loot isn't even on the Mahone Oak Island?

It is suggested that the legendary treasure will never be found in or near the famous Money Pit. Henry Sinclair or the Templars before him built the workings on the Mahone Oak Island with the intention of concealing a treasure there. But then, for some reason they changed their mind. Perhaps the Mahone island was abandoned because it was too easy to detect by ships crossing the Atlantic. Or perhaps, ships carrying treasure sailed into the Bay of Fundy by error and landed on the Minas Basin island—which then became the treasure island.

The possibility that a treasure awaits its discoverer on the Mahone Oak Island is, of course, not entirely ruled out. It is questionable if such a large project as that carried out on the Mahone Bay island would have really been "ditched." Perhaps, a great treasure was divided between the two islands. Henry Sinclair or the Templars before him may have avoided "putting all their eggs in one basket."

SOME HENRY SINCLAIR CASTLE enthusiasts feel that Nolan's Cross on the Mahone Oak Island suggests a religious connection with the Knight's Templar Order. Rather than doubloons and pieces of eight, the treasure may be of a religious nature. If there is a treasure on Oak

Island, at the Castle or on the Fundy island it may contain religious material of great significance for future generations.

Indeed, the Templars are believed to be the holders of a momentous secret from the Christian tradition. Indeed, we know that Templar-inspired secret societies exist today.

The authors of *The Holy Blood and the Holy Grail* advanced their theory on the alleged secret protected by the Templars. They suggest that a secret order behind the Knights Templar, known as the Prieure de Sion, functioned as the Templar's administrative arm. Although the original Knights Templar was dissolved between 1307 and 1312, the Prieure de Sion still exists today and manipulates critical Western development, and was instrumental in the direction of the domestic affairs of certain European countries. Furthermore, the objective of the Prieure de Sion was the restoration of a dynasty and bloodline to the thrones of France and other European nations. This bloodline had been guarded and kept a secret by the Templars with only a select few knowing the "truth." In this case, the "truth," rather than being a cup used by Christ at the Last Supper and by Joseph of Arimathea to collect drops of Jesus's blood at the crucifixion, the Holy Grail is a lineage, pedigree, or bloodline of people. The authors speculate that Jesus Christ was part of that bloodline, or married into it, fathering children and thus making the bloodline "holy." His wife (probably the Mary Magdalene from the village of Migdal or Magdale, in Galilee) and children fled the Holy Land and found refuge in Southern France where they preserved their lineage.

By 1100 Jesus's descendants had risen to great prominence in Europe and in Palestine. They were aware of their pedigree and ancestry but did not have the proof necessary for their future objectives, whatever they may have been. That proof lay buried beneath the Temple of Solomon. The Knights Templar's original mission was to find it.

A mid-twelfth-century pilgrim to the Holy Land, Johann von Wuzburg, reported stables beneath the Temple large enough to accommodate two thousand horses. In fact, the Knights Templar quartered their horses in these stables. It is theorized that the stables were built following a huge excavation by the Templars, during which they found what they were looking for and brought it back to Europe for concealment. About what was concealed, the authors of *The Holy Blood and The Holy Grail* write, "It may have been Jesus's mummified body. It may have been the equivalent, so to speak, of Jesus's marriage licence, and/or the birth certificates of his children.

It may have been something of comparable explosive import. Any or all of these items might have been referred to as the Holy Grail." What happened to the Templar's find remains a mystery.

The Sinclair castle enthusiasts who espouse the religious connection believe that the answer to the Holy Grail mystery may lay hidden beneath the oaks on the Fundy Oak Island.

ONE SUNNY MORNING in early September, I parked my car near the grove of oak trees which marks the original location of the Fundy Oak Island and followed the narrow trail out to the dyke, some 1,000

Dyke holding back the tides from the original Oak Island.

ft. from the oak grove. I walked another 1,000 ft. or so along the top of the dyke towards the mouth of the Gaspereau River, where I stopped to take a couple of pictures. As I gazed across the expanse of hayfield which was once under water and now separates the grove from the dyke, it occurred to me that the elevation of the top of the dyke was probably not far off that of the deck of a sailing ship. An ancient mariner may have also stood where I was standing while searching for the river. Looking across the hayfield at what was once a tiny oak-treed island, I was struck by how distinctly the oak grove stood out from what once was the original mainland. This tiny Fundy Oak Island was sufficiently far out to sea that it sharply contrasted with the treed hills in the far distant background. All of this may be strictly speculative but I had to ask myself, "Could it be really true? Was this really a signpost island? And, was something absolutely mind-boggling buried on this island?"

I told myself that this book was starting to get to me and walked back to my car. But, before I climbed in a farmer drove up on his tractor and cut the motor. He had eyed me making my way back along the trail and, noticing the camera around my neck, became curious. I explained my presence. I was writing a book, and I was there to take pictures and had been granted permission to do so. But, the farmer, wasn't concerned about "permissions." He was interested

The Fundy Oak Island is in the background of this photo taken from the dyke.

in the island from the perspective of the Henry Sinclair and Templar speculations. "They say that there's treasure buried on that piece of land," he said, nodding to the oak grove. I told my story to him much as you find it in this chapter. When I was through, this obviously "down to earth" gentleman remarked, "It may be true, you never know. This world is full of some of the most damned crazy things!"

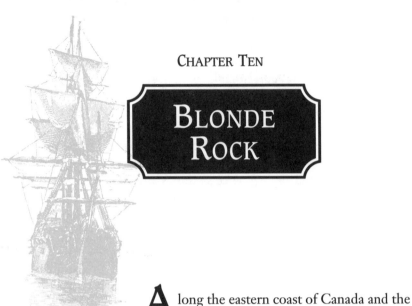

CHAPTER TEN

BLONDE ROCK

A long the eastern coast of Canada and the United States there are many rocks and ledges which have gained respect and fear due to the large number of ships they have claimed. A rock belonging to a list of these places of doom is situated near the largest of a string of islands that jut out into the Atlantic from the southeastern end of Nova Scotia like the tail of a giant kite. This rock is known to mariners as Blonde Rock. The island that is home to this ominous place of death and destruction is called Seal Island, situated about 20 mi. west of Cape Sable Island. Seal Island is about 2³/⁴ mi. long by about 1/2 mi. wide.

Blonde Rock, where hundreds of people have lost their lives in an untold number of shipwrecks, is situated about 3¹/² mi. off the southern end of Seal Island in a southeasterly direction. It is a vicious ledge of rock, extending some distance under water in a north and south direction and protruding above the water at normal low tides but is covered by water at high tides. Although the ledge is well marked by buoys in these modern days, ocean liners are nonetheless leery of the danger it imposes and stay well out to sea when passing the island.

The rock received its name from His Majesty's frigate *Blonde* that met her doom on this ill-fated ledge in 1782, during the War of American Independence. While cruising the New England coast, the *Blonde* captured the American vessel *Lion*, commanded by a Captain Tuck, bound from Massachusetts to Cadiz with a cargo of masts and spars. This load of marine equipment was a valuable prize for the King's navy so no time was wasted. Captain Tuck and his sixty-man crew of the *Lion* were taken on board the *Blonde* as prisoners. The

Lion was re-crewed with British seamen, and sent directly on ahead to the British headquarters at Halifax.

In the meantime, Captain Thornborough of the *Blonde* took his time crossing the mouth of the Bay of Fundy. It may be that he was searching for another prize or was expecting more encounters so took time out to press some of the *Lion's* crew into British Naval service to shore up his manpower.

It is not known if the *Blonde* was caught in a storm and blown off course, or if Captain Thornborough made a mistake in navigation or was just neglectful—perhaps paying too much attention to his captives and not enough to the sea. Whatever the reason, the *Blonde* struck the infamous ridge off Seal Island and began to sink.

The captain, crew, and prisoners took to the life boats and managed to reach Brig Rock on Seal Island. They probably had salvaged food from the foundering ship and planned to set up camp for their crew and prisoners while the captain and a few of his men struck out for Cape Sable or Yarmouth in their boats. However, to their surprise, the island had other visitors.

Two American privateer vessels, *Lively* and *Scammell*, lay at anchor in a secluded cove near the southern end of the island. Their masters, Captains Daniel Adams of Salem and Noah Stoddard of Boston, had found firewood and drinking water on the island. It provided an isolated hiding place in enemy territory. So, they anchored here frequently.

Captain Thornborough realized that his chance of winning a battle against the privateering crews with his much reduced manpower while keeping sixty Yankee prisoners in check were slim. So he decided to bargain. He proposed to the privateers that he would release Captain Tuck and the sixty American prisoners, along with a written guarantee of safe conduct to Salem, in return for the safe passage of himself and his British crew to Yarmouth. Captain Thorborough may have disguised his numbers, but that notwithstanding, the privateers probably didn't think that a bloody showdown was of any value to them. The Yankee captains agreed but on one condition. The British crew would have to relinquish their weapons. Captains Lively and Stoddard apparently didn't trust the British captain completely, or they just wanted to play it safe.

There is a freshwater pond behind Brig Rock, backed by a high ridge of beach stones. Here, Captain Thornborough chose an area beside the pond and lined up his crew. As Captains Adams and Stoddard, their men, and the liberated prisoners stood by and watched, the British sailors marched past the pond and threw their muskets, pistols, and cutlasses into its centre.

As promised, Captain Thornborough and his men were put ashore at Yarmouth and taken aboard a small Nova Scotia vessel, *Observer*, which set sail for Halifax. During the voyage, the *Observer* was preyed upon by an American privateer, the *Jack*, out of Salem. The smallness of the *Observer* belied the number on board. She carried over 173 men, all experienced in warfare. The captain of the *Jack* and his crew had taken on more than their match. After a relatively short battle, the British sailors boarded the *Jack*, and sailed her to Halifax. But, the captain and crew of the *Jack* were not held captive. Captain Thornborough set them free in an act of goodwill and appreciation for the fair treatment afforded him and his crew by the Yankee privateers.

Today, the pond into which the British tossed their weapons is known as Brig Rock Pond and the weapons may still be there. Recently, divers from Yarmouth searched its oceanside waters for the weapons, but they found nothing. The divers and others theorize that the action of the waves against the shore over many years has pushed the beach backward and the pond has become smaller. They suggest that the muskets, pistols and swords are covered with tons of beach stone. Perhaps the pond is smaller than when the *Blonde* sank, and perhaps the beach has moved landward. But, I doubt that the weapons are covered with "tons" of beach stones. I like to think that the muskets and other weapons will someday be recovered.

But there is more. The story is told that Captain Thornborough of the *Blonde* buried his treasure chest and bottles of Jamaican rum in the slopes around Brig Rock Pond. These stories sparked the imagination of the youths who lived on the island several decades ago. They searched relentlessly without finding the treasure chest. But, they did find several eighteenth-century bottles. Of course the corks had rotted away and the rum was gone, but if the bottles belonged to Captain Thornborough, surely his chest of gold and silver is nearby.

As for the *Blonde*, her remains must be near the rock that bears her name. She must lay there, cannons, fittings, and personal effects in place, perhaps even a pay chest.

THE NUMBER OF SHIPS lost to the ill-fated Blonde Rock is unknown. In the early 1800s people of the mainland used to sail out to Seal Island after a bad storm to bury the dead, but it was not until a lifesaving station was established on the island that an accurate record of casualties could be kept.

In his renowned and well-researched book *Shipwrecks of Nova Scotia, Volume 1*, Jack Zinck writes that before there was a lighthouse built on Seal Island, "some ninety-five wrecks occurred in and around the island." I suspect that Blonde Rock took a healthy percentage.

In 1824, two families, the Hichens and the Crowells, settled on the island and built houses after spending the first winter on the island in an old fishing shanty. There, they administered to the needs of shipwrecked sailors who were fortunate enough to reach the shores.

The Hichens and the Crowells petitioned for a lighthouse to be built on the island to warn ships of the dangers of Blonde Rock and other nearby shoals, and in 1831 a lighthouse was completed. It was built on an elevation 35 ft. above sea level. The light, 67 ft. above the ground, could be seen up to 16 mi. across the water. Despite the help of the lighthouse, the wrecks continued.

One of the most famous ships to meet her fate on Blonde Rock after the lighthouse was built was the clipper *Staffordshire*. She was built by the renowned shipbuilder from Nova Scotia, Donald McKay, in his East Boston yards for Enoch Train of the White Diamond line

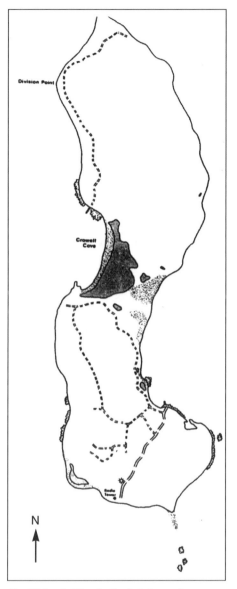

Seal Island. Blonde Rock is located 3½ mi. south of the lower tip of Seal Island.

of packets. The *Staffordshire* was en route from Liverpool, England, to Boston, carrying a mixed cargo and about three hundred passengers, when she ran into a fierce storm off the Nova Scotia coast and hit

Blonde Rock on the evening of December 29, 1853.

Rising high out of the water, the *Staffordshire* lurched and then slid back into the sea and floated free. But she lost her rudder and sprang a leak from the impact. Rudderless and taking in water, she drifted helplessly for hours before sinking. All were drowned except twenty-four crewmen and a twenty-five-year-old female passenger. They managed to escape the wreck in three lifeboats before she sank. The captain chose to go down with the ship. The survivors made it safely to the mainland. Two boats landed on or near Cape Sable Island while the third landed at Shelburne, about 30 mi. up the coast.

It is not known why only seamen rather than passengers, except for the woman, escaped from the wreck. It has been suggested that lack of discipline was to blame; that the crew deliberated too long on abandoning ship and panicked at the last moment, attending only to themselves and letting the passengers go down with the ship.

It is rumoured that there was gold in the ship's hold. However, even if the vessel didn't carry a load of bullion, there must have been a fortune in valuables belonging to the passengers that went down in the purser's safe.

OTHER SHIPS OF FAME carrying valuable cargos that were wrecked on Blonde Rock during the recorded history of Seal Island were the steamers *Ottawa* and *Assay*.

The *Ottawa*, owned by Christopher Furness, was built by Alex Stephen and Son of Linthouse, Glasgow, and christened in January 1891. The sleek and shiny steamer was 285 ft. long by 35 ft. wide, with a depth of 24 ft. She was schooner rigged but when not sailing under canvas, propelled by 25-horsepower steam engines. She was registered at 1,145 tons.

The *Ottawa* was crossing the Atlantic in the fall of the year of her christening, bound for Saint John, New Brunswick, when she drifted off course in bad weather and struck Blonde Rock. Her bow became lodged on the ledge and, unable to move, she filled with water. The ship was doomed.

The captain had no alternative but to abandon the ship which carried 300 tons of general cargo and a crew of twenty-six people. All were men except the stewardess, Annie Lindsey.

The lifeboats were lowered and all the crew got off the sinking ship before she went down. After watching the steamer disappear beneath the waves, they rowed toward Seal Island. Part way there, one of the boats carrying the stewardess and three men, overturned in the rough sea. Two of the men managed to swim in the freezing cold water to another boat and were pulled on board but by the time the capsized boat could be reached, the stewardess had drowned. The remaining man, who had clung to the bottom of the boat, was saved. Several hours later, the survivors reached Seal Island.

The *Assay* was a four-masted steamer which was commissioned to be built in 1891 by Elder Dempston and Company of Liverpool, England. Much larger than the *Ottawa*, she was registered in at 3,981 tons with the capacity to carry a large cargo.

The steamer set sail from Liverpool, England, for Saint John, New Brunswick on March 23, 1897. She carried 2,000 tons of valuable cargo—dry goods, carving sets, etc.—referred to as "Victoria Diamond Jubilee" merchandise.

The first part of the voyage passed without difficulty, but after five days out, the ship began to experience high seas and by March 30 was fighting a fierce storm. Deck fittings were torn off, the upper tower bridge was badly damaged, and two lifeboats swept away, leaving only three.

The next day brought calmer seas followed by fine weather and a brisk breeze. Good weather prevailed for the next four days but on April 5 brought poor visibility. The captain determined that they had passed Cape Sable but was unsure how close they were to Seal Island.

At midday, the *Assay* came to a grinding stop as she rode up on Blonde Rock, swung around and slammed broadside against the ledge. Hull plates cracked, gave way, and water began to flood the boiler room. The captain and his crew knew that their ship was doomed and fired a distress signal. Men crowded into the remaining three lifeboats and pushed away from the steamer while others huddled together near the bow to keep from being swept overboard. Meanwhile, help was on the way from Seal Island. A rescue boat manned by a lifesaving crew made it through rough seas and strong currents to the steamer and rescued all the stranded crew.

Writing about the wreck in his excellent book on the history and geography of Seal Island, *Island Trek*, Walter W. Hichens, the great-great-grandson of Richard and Mary Hichens, first settlers on the island, says, "Merchandise was strewn all along the Island's shore. Little English sailor suits for young boys, yards and yards of carpeting, broad cloth, trimmings for ladies apparel, bolts of brocaded satin, dozens of carving sets, sailor blouses for little girls and pleated skirts. All the women and girls of the island were the smartest dressed of any around at the time."

As testimony of the frequency at which the ill-fated Blonde Rock was capable of destroying vessels, one ship actually piled up on another. After the *Assay* crashed on the rock, she stayed there all summer and broke up in the fall storms but not before another ship encountered the ledge. The *Gerona*, bound from Portland to London, struck the wreck of the *Assay* and sank. The cargo, valued at over $250,000—a tidy sum in those days—was lost. By the grace of God, and the rescue men of Seal Island, the entire crew survived.

How many wrecks lie at the base of Blonde Rock? Over two centuries after the arrival of the first settlers from Europe, to the building of a lighthouse on Seal Island, thousands of ships plied up and down the eastern seaboard, passing Blonde Rock. Jack Zinck states that, "Before the time of their arrival [the Hichens and the Crowells] on this island, there had been an average of one wreck every twelve months." Although Zinck refers to Seal Island in general with Blonde Rock and other shoals off its shores, Blonde Rock was the island's major wrecker.

Over those centuries from early colonial times, ships departed ports of Europe for the New World, never to arrive. Some were most assuredly wrecked on Blonde Rock. French pay ships bound for Louisbourg and Quebec and British pay ships en route to Halifax may have been blown off course and wrecked on this jagged shoal. Spanish galleons loaded with treasure passed within a few hundred miles of Nova Scotia while following the Gulf Stream on their voyages from the Caribbean to home ports. Some may have been caught in the notorious Atlantic storms and driven northward.

At the foot of the rugged ledge called Blonde Rock, along with the *Blonde*, the *Ottawa*, and the *Assay*, and scores of other wrecks, there may lie a Spanish galleon; the stuff of the treasure hunter's dreams. It may lie there waiting for that adventurer with the imagination, patience, and financial resources to scoop up her hidden horde.

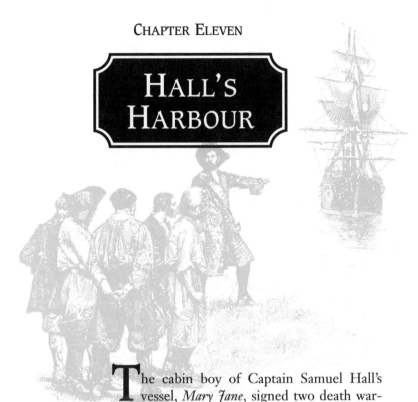

CHAPTER ELEVEN

HALL'S HARBOUR

The cabin boy of Captain Samuel Hall's vessel, *Mary Jane*, signed two death warrants the day he fell in love. He had met and fallen for an Indian maiden, the daughter of a tribal chief. The victims would be himself and his new-found love.

Little did the cabin boy and his Indian sweetheart know when they awoke at dawn one day in the late spring of 1779 that this would be their last day. And, little did they know that their deaths would mark the beginning of an extended treasure hunt: a search for lost treasure that continues today.

The cabin boy met his sweetheart on one of Captain Hall's frequent visits to a little Nova Scotia harbour in the Bay of Fundy, near the mouth of a small brook that spills out of North Mountain in the Annapolis Valley. The brook and the harbour now bear the Captain's last name. The name is an ominous reminder of sinister deeds because Captain Hall wrought terror in the hearts of valley settlers on the south side of the mountain opposite the harbour. With a pirate crew from the revolting New England colonies, he would cross over the mountain in the evening and swoop down on the unsuspecting valley residents in the wee hours of the morning, pillaging them, farm by farm.

Hall's Harbour, on the north side of the mountain, is about 10 mi. from the town of Kentville and a popular tourist attraction because of its scenic fishing village atmosphere and excellent lobster market. It is also of interest to those with a flair for the historical romance of piracy because Captain Samuel Hall, commander of the raiding ship *Mary Jane* frequently chose to anchor here between forays in the late years of the 1700s.

Although not exceptionally well sheltered, the harbour offered privateer Captain Hall and his marauders privacy as there were no settlers there. It provided an alternative to sailing into the populated Minas Basin where he would have been spotted by the residents who might have reported the ship's presence to the authorities in Halifax. It was a safe anchorage for the *Mary Jane*. Frequent fogs in the snug little harbour hid his much-wanted vessel from ships-of-war whose masters would have liked nothing better than to capture him and his pirate gang. Also, the nearest village lay in the valley on the opposite side of the mountain; far enough away that there was little fear of the *Mary Jane*'s arrival being noticed by a villager.

An Indian encampment between the harbour and the village provided still further security. Captain Hall won the Indians' support by handing out much desired gifts such as iron cooking pots, hatchets, iron arrow points, and blankets along with an array of cheap glittering jewellery. In return they agreed to report any villager who might cross over the mountain and see the vessel at anchor in the harbour.

The villagers in the valley were a hard-working and thrifty lot. Their splendid barns and chicken coops teamed with livestock and their root cellars were always well-stocked with vegetables for the long cold winter months. And they were generous, for they often shared the products of their labour with the Indians when hunting was hampered by deep snow. Captain Hall took advantage of this situation. As well as protecting the *Mary Jane* from detection, he had the Indians serve another purpose. As they were accustomed to visiting the villagers and begging for food during the cold winter months, he had them take note of where ample supplies were stored. They passed this information on to Captain Hall who used it well.

Twice, Captain Hall and his band of marauders sneaked over the mountain and pounced on the unsuspecting village people, carrying away their hard-earned food supplies. Each time, he stocked the *Mary Jane* with the ill-gotten gain and sailed off to plunder commercial ships on the high seas. But the advantage he had over the pillaged settlers was not to endure.

Two raids by Captain Hall were more than the valley populace could bear. Something had to be done before the pirates struck again. The villagers suspected that the Indians had provided Captain Hall with information on their food supplies in exchange for gifts. But what could be done? They knew that threatening the Indians with violence would be foolish. It wouldn't win them over to their side. But they knew that "you can catch more flies with honey than with a stick." So, they simply offered more than Captain Hall could give. The better bribe required that the Indians immediately notify the villagers when the *Mary Jane* again arrived in the harbour and assist with an attack on Captain Hall and his culprits. A winter's food supply far outweighed anything so far handed out by Captain Hall. The Indians agreed.

CAPTAIN HALL was aware of his cabin boy's romance with the Indian chief's daughter. He knew that the boy would be anxious to visit the Indian encampment as soon as possible each time the *Mary Jane* dropped anchor in the harbour. Therefore, he seized the opportunity to use the boy as a messenger. The cabin boy's presence in the encampment signalled the ship's arrival; he would be asked if supplies on the ship were down, if Captain Hall had gifts to distribute, if the captain had instructions for the chief, and so on.

As well as being in love with the Indian maiden, the cabin boy had become a close friend of her younger brother. The two boys played games and exchanged knowledge. What one boy knew was a mystery to the other. Indeed, it was a happy time for the cabin boy, the maiden, and her brother whenever the *Mary Jane* sailed into the harbour and dropped anchor. But those happy days were not to last.

On that fateful day in the late spring of 1779, Captain Samuel Hall and his cut-throat crew slid into the harbour for a few days of rest from plunder on the high seas. A lookout reported the arrival of the *Mary Jane* to the Indian chief who immediately sent his daughter off to notify the villagers. In view of the relationship of the chief's daughter and son with the cabin boy, neither had been told of the change of heart towards Captain Hall. As she hurried towards the village, she wondered why her father had dispatched her to warn the villagers of the return of the ship on which her lover had just arrived. But, as a woman of the tribe, it was not her place to ask questions, so she ran her errand knowing that the cabin boy from the *Mary Jane* would arrive at the encampment while she was gone, and hoping that he would still be there when she returned. In the meantime, the cabin boy arrived looking for his sweetheart. He told the chief that the *Mary Jane* was short on food supplies, that an attack on the village was to be undertaken that evening, and received information on the best stocked barns. Then he waited for his maiden. Several hours elapsed but his love did not return. Finally, when he could wait no longer, he told the maiden's brother to tell his sister that he would be alone on the *Mary Jane* that evening during the attack and for her to meet him on the shore.

At dusk, the maiden returned hoping that her lover would still be there. When she found that he had left, she cried bitter tears, until her brother told her that she was to go down to the harbour and meet the cabin boy on the shore. She hurried down the mountainside to meet her lover who was waiting for her on the beach opposite where the *Mary Jane* lay at anchor.

Meanwhile, the maiden's brother happened to overhear the men discussing a raid on Captain Hall and his crew by the settlers, and it was to take place that very evening! The settlers had been tipped off by the chief's daughter, and Captain Hall and his men were to be ambushed on their way over the hills to the village. This was shocking news and the boy became concerned for the safety of his sister and his friend.

The Indian boy waited for his chance while the men became engrossed in storytelling around the camp fire; during a moment of great hilarity, the boy slipped out of the camp unnoticed and raced over the hills toward the harbour.

As he approached the shore, he heard the men from the *Mary Jane* making their way up the hillside from the beach; there was no need for silence until they passed the Indian encampment. He rushed into their midst, grabbed Captain Hall by the arm and rapidly told him of the trap that had been set to capture and kill him and his men. But the boy was too late.

Assisted by a couple of Indian guides, the settlers had skilfully manoeuvred themselves behind the advancing pirates. Concealed by the pirate gang's noisy trekking through the bush, they had silently crept between them and the ship. Shots rang out, piercing the tranquillity of the night. Realizing that they were far outnumbered by the villagers, Hall and his ratty followers broke rank and ran for cover into the surrounding woods.

The settlers followed them into the forest, and as they searched the thickets, the Indian boy skilfully led the pirates around to the rear of their pursuers. Meanwhile, another party of settlers from the village were making their way down the hillside towards the *Mary Jane*. They were determined to catch and kill Captain Hall and his merry band of cut-throats.

As he had done on previous raids, Captain Hall had left his cabin boy in charge of the ship's treasure chest which the boy had been told was filled with gold. The instructions that night were the same as before. If Captain Hall and his men should not return by a certain time, the cabin boy was to put the chest ashore and bury it in the sands close to the edge of the woods. If the captain nor any of the ship's crew should fail to return, the treasure would be his in reward for his trustworthiness.

When the sounds of gunfire rang out from the woods beyond the beach, the cabin boy knew that something had gone drastically wrong. His pirate buddies obviously were under attack. In keeping with Captain Hall's concern for the treasure chest, he and the Indian maiden lowered it down with ropes into a rowboat and landed it on the shore. Then they lugged it up to the edge of the beach, scooped out a hole in the ground, and as quickly as possible, dropped it in and covered it over with the excess soil.

As the cabin boy and the Indian girl hurried back to where they had hauled the rowboat ashore, some of the ambushers heard their footsteps on the beach stones and opened fire. Both the boy and his Indian sweetheart were shot to death before they could reach the water.

Meanwhile, the settlers continued to search the woods for the pirate gang but they never found them. The Indian boy cleverly guided the marauders away from the searching settlers to their vessel. Without waiting to determine the whereabouts of the cabin boy or the chest of gold, Captain Hall and his pillaging crew hastily pulled anchor and sailed out of the harbour, never to return.

The chest of gold has never been found!

CHAPTER TWELVE

THE
TREASURE WELL
OF CARIBOU ISLAND

In 1497, John Cabot landed on Nova Scotia's Cape Breton Island and planted the British flag, claiming Atlantic Canada for the English. Following this act of possession, the French attempted to establish ownership and Samuel de Champlain established a permanent French settlement at Port Royal, on the Bay of Fundy, in 1605. Then, in 1621, the British laid claim to the territory on the argument that Cabot was the first to plant a flag. For nearly a century-and-a-half, England and France waged wars over ownership of this part of the new world.

By 1713, France had lost most of her colonies in Atlantic Canada, retaining only the islands of Prince Edward, Cape Breton, St. Pierre, and Miquelon. In 1719, to defend what remained and to protect commercial interests in the new world, the French began construction of the enormous fortress of Louisbourg near the eastern tip of Cape Breton Island.

The fortress was huge, covering about 50 acres of land surrounding the town of Louisbourg. It was built by engineers, artisans, and private contractors from France and was completed in 1744 at a cost of millions of dollars.

Louisbourg was one of the busiest ports on the Atlantic seaboard. It constituted an important link between France and the French West Indies sugar plantations. And, it required a lot of money. So much, that some officials of the day described Louisbourg as "a bottomless pit for funds" and the King of France is said to have remarked, "the streets of Louisbourg must be paved with gold." During and after its construction, pay ships brought gold and silver from France to supply the coffers of the colonial governor in Quebec and to pay military troops and construction workers.

The year after Louisbourg was completed, France and Britain were at war again and the British captured Louisbourg after a forty-nine-day siege. During the siege, the port of Louisbourg was blockaded by the British, although some French ships did slip through during the darkness of night while others successfully bypassed the blockade. According to legend, one vessel that managed to bypass the blockade was a pay ship from France, which slipped through the Strait of Canso—the 1-mi. wide strip of water separating Cape Breton Island from mainland Nova Scotia.

The plan may have been to sail clockwise around the island and deliver the money to Louisbourg from a nearby unguarded harbour, or the ship may have headed for Quebec as French ships en route for that city sailed through the Strait of Canso. Whichever, the pay ship never reached its destination. It was blown off course in a storm and wrecked on Gull Rock off Caribou Harbour, west of Pictou Harbour.

Some or all of the ship's crew survived and managed to unload the gold and silver into boats and land it on Caribou Island. There, on a sandy beach, the survivors dug a large pit, dubbed the Treasure Well, lined it with stones and shovelled in the loot.

Then, the sailors struck off for the mainland with the hope of meeting up with some of their own people or finding refuge with friendly Indians. But their plight failed when they were captured on the mainland by the British, taken to the Halifax garrison and thrown into prison.

Today, after more than 250 years of shoreline erosion, the Treasure Well is thought to lie somewhere below the level of low tide.

ONE WARM MONDAY MORNING in late August, I decided to check out the legend and headed for Caribou Island. On the drive from Halifax, I thought about the Treasure Well and wondered if the trip would prove to be nothing short of a "wild goose chase." What did I expect to learn? Would the residents of the island know anything about the legend? And, if they did, how could they be expected to know or even guess where the payload might be stashed? Surely there were numerous places. I had never been to Caribou Island but according to my road map it stretched over 4 mi. into the Northumberland Strait— about six times the length of the Oak Island of Money Pit fame. Opinions differ as to where the long sought treasure is situated on that relatively large island. What hope was there of finding anything on Caribou Island?

Anxiety set in as the miles rolled by. How would I approach the people on the island? What would be the reaction if I knocked on a country kitchen door and asked, "I wonder if you can help me? I'm checking out the story of a lost legendary treasure known as the Treasure Well of Caribou Island." Surely, I would have to work out a better approach than that.

My thoughts turned to those sailors who reputedly buried the treasure. How many might have been involved? Six, ten, fifty? If all or most survived the wreck, the number of mariners involved might have been large. Wouldn't one or more of the crew have returned to retrieve the treasure?

One answer loomed large: lack of opportunity. The war between Britain and France was temporarily put to rest in 1748 by the Treaty of Aix-la-Chapelle but raged again ten years later. The pay ship crew who were captured by the British probably found themselves back crewing on French ships three years after the shipwreck. Fifteen years passed before hostilities ended with the Peace of Paris. Some of the shipwreck survivors may have died in battle, of illness or of old age before the war finally ended. And, of those who may have survived the war, getting up an expedition to retrieve the treasure would have been an expensive and trying task.

After the Peace of Paris, about thirty years passed before settlers arrived on Caribou Island. The first to settle were Thomas Patterson and one Rogers. If any of the early settlers had searched for the treasure, they may have searched in vain. As I will explain later, shoreline erosion played a dramatic hand.

I don't make a practice of chasing legends, and wouldn't have given the Caribou Island tale more than a second thought except for the fact that pay ships did make trips to Louisbourg from France. Many vessels were lost on the Atlantic crossing and it is reasonable that some were pay ships. Furthermore, Caribou Island is on the early French colonial shipping route to Quebec. French ships en route for Quebec sailed through the Strait of Canso and passed by the island. And, some were pay ships. That one may have met its doom on treacherous Gull Rock seems plausible.

One pay ship, *Le Chameau*, floundered directly off Louisbourg in late August of 1725, six years following the commencement of the building of the fortress. She had crossed the Atlantic from France and was bound for Quebec with a stopover at Louisbourg.

Le Chameau was off course when she ran into an early fall storm, struck a reef and was completely demolished. All 316 people on board were drowned.

Le Chameau's payload was substantial. She carried 289,696 livres in gold and silver for the Canadian coffers. Wreckage strewed the beaches but not everything washed ashore. Part of the ship sank to the ocean floor at a location that left the wreck in shallow water at low tide.

A salvage operation of soldiers and sailors was immediately mounted and continued throughout the winter and into the summer but only about 6,000 livres were recovered for all their efforts. The unrecovered treasure, in addition to the gold and silver included expensive guns and fittings.

The reef where the pay ship broke up was named Chameau Rock and periodic searches were conducted in that general area for over two hundred years without success. Then, in 1965, a trio of Nova Scotians, Alex Storm, Dave MacEachern, and Harvey MacLeod, recovered the wreck following years of exhausting searches. The value of treasure found in that year of discovery was $250,000.

A PESSIMISTIC MOOD came over me after crossing the causeway to Caribou Island. Sign posts at the entrances of long driveways down to the sea gave the impression of summer homes and weekend cottages—not the old homes of long established residents whose grandparents or great-grandparents might have handed down a tale of lost treasure. About 1¹ᐟ² mi. beyond the causeway, the road skirted a beach on the north side of the island bearing a sign warning motorists of a penalty for driving off the beaten path and onto the shore. Could this be the site of the Treasure Well? My 1:50,000 scale map showed Gull Point at the far east end of the island. I presumed that Gull Rock was somewhere near Gull Point. I imagined the crew from the pay ship drifting with a gale from the north and struggling to a sheltered beach on the south side. I drove on.

About five minutes later, the road came to an abrupt stop at a lighthouse. This was the end of the island and Gull Point. Where was the beach of the Treasure Well? I recalled seeing a sign about 1/2 mi. back advertising "sailboats for sale." I would try to make a sensible enquiry at a place of business, where I could strike up a conversation and introduce my questions in a casual fashion.

Two German shepherds eyed me suspiciously as I drove up the driveway to the shop that sold the sailboats. I hesitated momentarily because of the dogs, then stepped out as they backed away and two smiling gentlemen walked from the shop to receive me.

I explained that I was in the throes of writing a book about buried treasure and shipwrecks and the like and it might include a chapter about their island. Then I quickly summarized what I had heard of the legend.

My hosts didn't seem surprised. One of them reached down to pat a shepherd on the head while the other said, "It's right there," and pointed to a well-box beside the road near the driveway entrance. "That's the treasure well." He was obviously joking but he sounded serious.

I explained that according to the legend, the Treasure Well was out beyond low tide. The shore appeared to be about 400 ft. south of the road.

Both men broke into smiles. I obviously knew what I was talking about and, yes, they had heard of the Treasure Well. "Just a moment," one of the men said, "you should be talking to Glen."

A moment later Glen Johnston, age thirty-five, strolled up to our little gathering. The more talkative man explained my quest to Glen.

"Follow me," Glen said, motioning to a bungalow near the sales office, "I may have some old photos that could be of help."

Glen introduced me to his wife Debby, explained my business on the island and started digging out photo albums. "There was a group of scientists over here a few years ago," Glen said as he paged through the album. "They went all over the ground at this end of the island with detectors but didn't find anything." However, Glen said he didn't think that the search eliminated the possibility that a treasure existed. He agreed with the opinion that the treasure was out beyond low tide. He spoke of his childhood years on the island and of hearing stories from his father. As to where the treasure might be, Glen had always understood that it was out beyond the beach opposite his house.

After looking at some old photographs of the area around his end of the island we went outside where Glen pointed out a particular location on the south shore, separated from the road by about 400 ft. of low level grassland, just opposite the well-box. Referring to an abrupt change in the direction of the shoreline, Glen was certain about the general location. "Not there, where the shore juts back towards the road but directly across from us." But, where was the sand beach? All I could see was green grass. The legend tells of a well dug in the sands of a beach. Glen explained that there was, indeed, a beach. It was hidden from view by a grassy ridge of sand and not visible from his house or the road.

After thanking Glen for his hospitality and information, I headed out for the beach to take a few photos. On my walk across the grassland between the road and the shore, I found myself ankle-deep in water. It occurred to me that I was walking in a meadow that might someday be invaded by the sea, if its level was in range of the tides. The significance of that thought would come later.

Hiking over the grassy ridge, I stepped onto the shore. More than 1,000 ft. of sand beach stretched out before me. The tide was at its highest for the day, and it was a "spring" tide. (A spring tide occurs when the sun and moon are in line and this occurs both on a full-moon and on a new moon. The "spring" has no reference to the seasons. At these times, high tides are higher and low tides are lower. Tidal ranges are at their least and called "neap" tides when the moon is in the first and last quarter.) Although the high tide was of the higher range, a substantial section of sand lay between the water's edge and the top of the grassy ridge. What I was looking at matched what I had imagined as the beach where the sailors dug their treasure pit: a sand beach sufficiently wide to provide an area to carry out the work of disposing of a ship's treasure.

Just before leaving the island, I visited an elderly lady, Helen Beard, who lived not far from the beach where the treasure is purportedly buried. Glen and Debby Johnston had recommended that I talk with her about the Treasure Well. Mrs. Beard was not disposed to go into details about the lost treasure. "If my husband was alive, he could tell you all about it," she said apologetically, explaining that she didn't profess to be an expert on the subject. However, she was helpful to the extent of confirming Glen's notion of the treasure location. "Over there, somewhere," Mrs. Beard declared, motioning in the general direction of the place pointed out by Glen.

THAT THE TREASURE is thought to lie somewhere below the level of low tide held no particular import the day that Glen Johnston pointed out the general location of the Treasure Well. It was not until a couple of weeks later when I was reviewing hydrographic charts that the significance of the "below low tide" theory bobbed its head above water. The chart showed a 1,500 ft. wide point of low land named Gull Spit jutting out over 3,000 ft. into Caribou Harbour beyond the line of high tide of the beach where I had stood that day snapping photos. It had been covered by the water of high tide when

I aimed my camera up and down the beach. Gull Spit is shown on the chart as above low tide. It was covered by the water of high tide when I visited the beach. The chart showed Gull Rock situated near the edge of low tide on Gull Point, placing it just north of the lighthouse.

To what extent had erosion from the pounding sea played a part in confusing the location? Did the beach once lie further out to sea? Had there once been another ridge of land supporting a beach far out on the present spit? And did the wet meadow between the beach and the sea once stretch out to meet another beach of yesterday? It is reasonable to imagine the pounding surf slowly and imperceptibly wearing away the existing beach, flooding the meadow and creating a new beach beside the road in front of Glen Johnston's house. Had a similar reshaping of the landscape occurred on a more seaward place after the Treasure Well was dug?

The lighthouse at Gull Point.

I looked to history for an answer and found it in *A History of the County of Pictou* by the Rev. George Patterson, 1877. The historian declares to have spared no effort in acquiring the information for his book, plodding his way through newspaper files and works of colonial history, ransacking the county and provincial records, corresponding extensively, visiting various parts of the county looking for facts and interrogating the Indians. The Reverend writes that he, "labored as conscientiously, as if he were writing the history of Europe," and "as the Scotch would say, 'expiscated' every old man and woman he has met within the country for years."

The history contains an undated map of Pictou County signed by Geo. Hattie, Land Surveyor, and reduced from a large map of A. F. Church and Company. On the map, Caribou (then spelled Carriboo) Island is called Big Caribou Island, Gull Point is called Caribou Point and the high and dry land of the point dog-legs south following the full course of the present-day Gull Spit. On this map, Munroes Island (Little Caribou) scales at a distance of only 1/2 mi. from Caribou Island.

Caribou Island was a headland connected to the shore when the first explorers arrived. They are said to have seen a herd of caribou on the east point of what is now Caribou Island, which they thence named Caribou Point.

Caribou Harbour has two principal entrances, one between Caribou Island and Munroes Island and another much narrower and

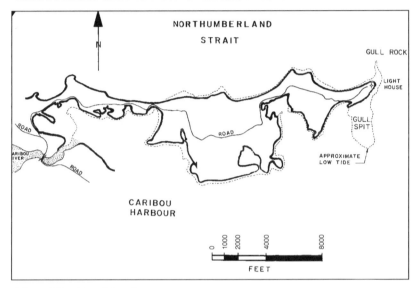

NORTHUMBERLAND STRAIT

GULL ROCK

LIGHT HOUSE

GULL SPIT

APPROXIMATE LOW TIDE

CARIBOU RIVER

ROAD

ROAD

ROAD

CARIBOU HARBOUR

0 1000 2000 4000 8000

FEET

Map of Caribou Island.

deeper between the latter and the mainland. The entrance between Caribou Island and Munroes Island accommodates the 14 mi. ferry run between Pictou and Wood Islands, Prince Edward Island. This well-used ferry entrance to Caribou Harbour did not exist a split second ago on the geological scale of time. It was a sand beach when the first settlers arrived, which the sea was beginning to erode away. Patterson writes, "It [the sea] has, however, continued its encroachments, till it has entirely separated between the two islands, making a passage 1/2 mi. wide with 4 ft. of water on it at low tide. Within the memory of the first settlers the sea has also cut across the beach, which connected what is now the Big [Carriboo] Island with the land, and thus formed a third entrance, which, however, is still shallow. And further changes are going on. At two if not three places on the

Big Island [Carriboo], which were once meadows, cutting considerable quantities of hay, are now only narrow sand beaches, which the sea is wearing away, and which will soon cut through, and thus convert into three or four islands."

Patterson, writing on or before 1877, was obviously a bit hasty in predicting that Caribou Island would "soon" be converted into "three or four islands" but the rate of erosion during his time and earlier must have prompted him to see a more rapid devastation. Indeed, the rate of change of the shorelines had been fast. The first

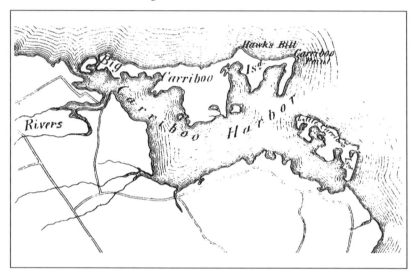

An excerpt from a map of the 1800s, showing Gull Spit as a prominent portion of Caribou Island. Note that Munroes Island is called Little Cariboo Island.

permanent settlers came to Pictou on a ship called the *Betsey* in 1767. During the following one hundred years these settlers and their descendants witnessed the sand beach connecting Caribou Island and Munroes Island wash away, leaving a 1/2 mi. wide passage between the islands. Of the erosion in general, Patterson writes, "Both inside and outside the harbours, it is being gradually worn away, the sandstone, which forms the underlying rock, readily yielding to the influence of the waves. At Middle River Point, those who can remember a period of about fifty years, estimate that in that time about 200 ft. of the shore has been carried away. The island there is not now half the size it was within their recollection, and a small island on the Middle River has in the same time been entirely carried away, except a few stones visible at low water. This washing goes on with greatest rapidity under the influence of northeast winds, which cause our highest tides, and drive the water with great force, particularly against the shores of the Harbour [Pictou Harbour]."

The components that lend credence to the legend of the Treasure Well are: a dangerous ledge named Gull Rock on the Colonial French shipping lane to Quebec; shipments of gold and silver to the money-hungry Canadian coffers; frequent shipwrecks including the pay ship *Le Chameau* off Louisbourg Harbour; disap-

Beach at Gull Spit above high tide. This beach once extended across to Munroes Island (left side of land on the horizon.)

pearing beaches. They all add up to give the legend a ring of reality. However, one part of the tale may have thrown those who may have searched for the treasure astray. It is the presumption that the treasure lays out beyond low tide.

The early settlers witnessed beaches literally disappear within their lifetimes, so rapid was the action of wind and sea. The collective memory of those who live near and on Caribou Island is that the treasure was lost to beach erosion. But was it? The first settlers may have carried out cursory searches and then lost interest in view of the disappearing shoreline. They may have been justified, but one aspect of the diminishing shoreline of Caribou Island bears scrutiny.

An examination of the modern hydrographic chart against old

maps of nineteenth-century vintage suggests that there has been little loss of shoreline in the vicinity of the most easterly tip of Caribou Island. You may note from the map of Caribou Island that the stubby finger of Gull Spit begins its seaward approach at a point about a 1/4 mi. southwest of the extremity of Gull Point. Could the legendary survivors of the wrecked pay ship have landed on this 1/4 mi. portion of shoreline? They lined their treasure pit with stones. Where did they get the rock? Did they gather stones from the forest bordering the shore?

Treed land at Gull Point is in the background where treasure may have been hidden. The beach at Gull Spit is in the foreground.

Having loaded the boats with the ship's cargo of gold, it is reasonable that the mariners sought shelter as soon as possible. Protection from the gale that wrecked their ship may have been found on this leeward side of the point, not far from Gull Rock, presuming that it was a north wind common to most storms of the area. This seems to be a more likely location than some windy place far out on the existing beach that joined the two islands.

Furthermore, the Treasure Well may not have been dug on the beach. Although legend says that the sailors buried the gold in the sand of a beach, it could be wrong. Perhaps the sailors chose a place to dig in the woods adjacent to the beach. Wouldn't that be more logical? Would you choose to bury a ship's cargo of gold in a hole in the sand or a more protected place among the trees beside the shore?

We need to think as those mariners would have thought. They had no idea when they might return, if ever. Their offspring might be the retrievers, or some other party might have to be engaged to return. Surely, they would have wanted to reference the place where they buried the treasure. Among the trees, there would have been something in the way of landmarks to note the deposit: say, ten paces south of a large spruce and twenty paces from the edge of the shore, or something of this nature.

All this speculation may seem far-fetched but without it there is little hope of ever finding the Treasure Well, if, indeed, it ever was dug. For after all, it is only a legend.

CHAPTER THIRTEEN

JOHN KEATING
AND
COCOS ISLAND

Like Oak Island, there are countless legends of vast treasures buried on Cocos Island off the west coast of Central America, and the most outstanding involves a Captain John Keating of St. John's, Newfoundland.

Cocos Island, a 20 mi. square speck of land some 3,000 mi. south of San Francisco and about 300 mi. south of Puntarenas, Costa Rica, has seen over 400 expeditions to her shores to recover reputed booty. Scores of searchers have worn their fingers to the bone digging, tunnelling, and blasting in search of fabulous caches of silver, gold, and jewels believed to have been buried by pirates of bygone days. The total dollar cost of the numerous expeditions over the years is estimated in the millions.

The famed loot of Lima is said to be the largest of all the treasures buried on Cocos Island, exceeding $60 million in gold and silver. As the story goes, government and church officials fled the city of Lima with the accumulated wealth of centuries during a South American revolution in the early 1800s. They fled to the seaport of Callao with their enemy in hot pursuit and piled their valuables in the fort.

A British ship, *Mary Dier* happened to be in the harbour and as an attack on the defenceless fort was expected at any time, the fugitives loaded the treasure on board the ship, believing that the enemy wouldn't dare attack a British vessel.

Among the vast horde of valuables thrust aboard were hundreds of bars of silver and gold, emerald studded crosses, carved gold plates

146

from the Inca civilization, and a life-size statue of the Madonna and child taken from the Cathedral of Lima. All the glittering wealth was too much for the ship's crew to resist, and that night they threw the Peruvian guards overboard and sailed out to sea.

The next morning the crew realized they were being chased by an armed vessel, but the *Mary Dier* was in tiptop shape and a fast craft. They hoisted every inch of canvas and outdistanced their pursuers. By the following morning, they were nowhere in sight.

But the thieves had another problem. What to do with their ill-gotten gains? Several ideas were kicked around until finally they decided to sail up the coast and bury the treasure on Cocos Island.

About two weeks later, the *Mary Dier* reached Cocos Island. The crew dropped anchor in one of the small harbours called Chatham Bay, ferried the loot ashore in ten boatloads, and piled it on the beach. Then they searched for a place to bury it. They found a piece of level land consisting of about 2 acres at the foot of a mountain just back from the shore where they had landed. They buried the treasure in boxes and hides near a stream running down from the mountain, being well aware that it was worth many millions.

The captain and crew of the *Mary Dier* didn't linger long on Cocos. After taking on a supply of fresh drinking water, they set sail for Panama to replenish their provisions.

On the fourth day out, they ran into a fierce gale that tore away most of the ship's rigging. After floating helplessly in the crippled ship for three days, they sighted land and decided to try to reach it in the long boat. But while they were lowering the boat, they were apprehended by a Peruvian ship. Eight of the eldest men of the *Mary Dier* were immediately shot and three of the youngest were spared to lead the Peruvians to the treasure. One of the three who escaped execution was a young lad of eighteen years by the name of Thompson. He had shipped on the *Mary Dier* earlier that year before it anchored in Callao and stole the Lima treasure.

The Peruvian ship didn't go directly to Cocos Island. The crew was suffering from a tropical disease and put into the Gulf of Panama to seek medical help. But many died, including one of the three young crew members of the *Mary Dier*. Thompson survived.

After three weeks, Thompson and his co-survivor decided to try to escape. They believed they had a good chance of getting away as the Peruvian ship on which they were being held was not well guarded due to the toll taken by the disease. They also knew that they would be shot after they had led the Peruvians to the treasure so any attempt at getting away was better than staying put, even if it meant swimming in shark-infested waters.

A British whaler, the barque *James Morris* lay anchored about a mile off. It was worth a try. So, under cover of night they slithered silently down the anchor cable and swam unnoticed over to the whaler where they were congenially received by the man on watch. He gave them clothes, water, and food, and hid them in a barrel in the ship's hold where they stayed for almost a week until the whaler pulled anchor and slipped out of port.

A soon as the whaler was underway, Thompson and his fellow stowaway appeared on deck where they were signed on to serve as members of the ship's crew.

The *James Morris* crossed over to Hawaii and dropped anchor in a busy port where Thompson's buddy jumped ship. Thompson stayed with the whaler until it arrived at New Bedford, Massachusetts, where he signed off.

From New Bedford, Thompson crewed on another ship to Havana, Cuba, where he met a man by the name of John Keating of St. John's, Newfoundland. Thompson asked Keating if his skipper, Captain Humphreys, would take on another hand. Keating approached the captain and Thompson was taken aboard.

On the voyage back to Newfoundland, Thompson told his new friend Keating about the treasure. He suggested that if Keating could find a backer in St. John's to fit out a vessel, they could sail around the Horn to the island and recover the horde.

Back in St. John's, Keating approached two prominent merchants, a Captain Boag and a Mr. Pretcherd, who agreed to hear Thompson's proposal. Captain Boag found Thompson's story credible and the proposal feasible but neither could come up with the money at the moment. They told Thompson and Keating to be patient.

Thompson stayed with Keating for three months until a rumour spread about town that he, Thompson, was a pirate. Afraid of being arrested, Thompson slipped onto a ship bound for London, England. From there he wrote a letter asking Keatng to come and see him.

Keating informed Captain Boag of Thompson's urgent request, and the two men decided to see him. In London, they met with Thompson, but apparently no arrangement to join company in a voyage to Cocos was consummated. Keating and Captain Boag returned home and Thompson shipped off to Calcutta and was never seen or hard from again.

Back in St. John's, the two merchants fitted out a vessel and Keating and Boag took half a shipload of dried fish to a Caribbean port, where they waited for six weeks for another captain by the name of Gault to join them. Then they set sail for Cocos, apparently without Gault knowing the reason for the voyage.

The voyage went very badly. The two captains had a falling out and exchanged insults. Discontent developed among the men and the crew mutinied, throwing their support behind Captain Gault.

Captain Boag and Keating struck an agreement between themselves. They would hand over the vessel to Captain Gault, providing he would let them go ashore on Cocos Island to have a look around. Then they would have the crew drop them off at Panama where they would acquire their own vessel and go back to Cocos.

When they reached the island, Keating and Boag had little trouble finding the treasure. Obviously, Thompson had been specific with his information to Keating. They found the treasure in a cave near the stream, hidden from view by tall grass. In a statement purportedly made on August 6, 1882, Keating described the location: "The grass grows high on this level, when you are at it you cannot see it [the entrance]. I was a good while before I found it; my back was resting against the stone that formed the door."

Captain Boag cautioned Keating to only take out as much as they could conceal in their clothing. In this way, they were able to board the vessel with some of the booty. No one on the ship suspected that they had found the treasure.

A short time later, they sailed for Panama, where the ship dropped anchor and Captain Boag and Keating made off to shore alone in a boat. Part way there, the boat capsized and Boag was drowned while Keating was rescued by Gault.

Soon after, Keating and Captain Gault went their separate ways. Gault sailed off to a group of islands known to Keating as the "Pearl Islands" for a load of pearl shells. Keating hired two mules and a guide and crossed the Panama isthmus to the Caribbean. He arrived back home in St. John's, Newfoundland, a couple of months later.

While he was there, Keating drew a rough map of Cocos Island as there were no charts available at that time. He noted on the map where Gault had anchored and where he and Boag had found treasure.

According to my information, Keating died in 1882. On his deathbed he drew up another map of the island from memory and made a statement, dated August 6, 1882, which bears his signature and the names Matthew Henderson and John Phillips, witnesses to the signing of the documents. He refers to the treasure site, "On the map you will find marked No. 1 means a cave ..." and, after describing the site as I previously quoted, Keating provides some rather confusing information.

"I took away the stone and took £1,300, which I concealed in my clothes. I replaced the stone back in its own place as I found it and left it the same as I did four years before.

"There was no person with me at the time. I left the vessel this day alone and I returned to the vessel, no person knew that I had found the money, if they did my life would have been in great danger. They said they would take my life if I did not share equal. When I heard this it put me on my guard so I kept all a secret.

"On No. 2 marked on the map, a place called Morgan's Point, are $5 million worth buried. By the side of the river in Anchorage Bay are three pots of gold coin. I could not bring it to bear to go the third time.

"This is my last and full statement, so help me God."

From the statement I take it that either Keating returned to Cocos again four years after his visit with Captain Boag or he mistakenly wrote "years" for "days." From his comment on the danger of being caught with "the money" and "I could not bring it to bear to go the third time" it seems that the latter is more likely and Keating sneaked back alone and took a second helping of the pie.

Robert I. Nesmith who wrote the book *Dig for Pirate Treasure*, published in 1959, writes, "The North Sydney, Newfoundland, Herald of December 1, 1880, carried this item: 'This is to certify that I have given to Thomas Hackett all the papers and all the information that I ever possessed necessary to find the treasure buried on Cocos Island, and that Richard Young nor anyone else has any information that will help them find to the said treasure.

Signed: John Keating   Witness: Geo. B. Ingraham

These papers came into the hands of Captain Fred M. Hackett, a brother of Thomas, in the year 1890." Apparently, Keating had arranged a trip with Thomas Hackett in 1880 but according to Nesmith, Hackett "died of yellow fever in Havana before sailing."

What happened to Keating's maps? Perhaps they are somewhere in a trunk in someone's attic, somewhere in St. John's, Newfoundland!

CHAPTER FOURTEEN

GRAVEYARD OF THE GULF

About 15 mi. off the most northern tip of Cape Breton Island, Nova Scotia, lies a small but rugged parcel of land known as St. Paul Island. Frequently shrouded in fog, it waits to devour any ship that ventures too close to its jagged rocks. Situated in the Cabot Strait, the body of water separating Newfoundland from Cape Breton, it lies directly in the path of ships sailing to and from the Gulf of St. Lawrence and has claimed more than its share of wrecks. Like Sable Island which has earned the nickname "Graveyard of the Atlantic," St. Paul is frequently called "The Graveyard of the Gulf."

The waters surrounding the island are treacherous. Rocks with surgically sharp edges lie just below the surface. The island's rocky masses rise to heights of more than 400 ft. Its cliffs are nearly vertical and surrounded by deep water. In bygone days when a vessel would crash against the rocks in fog, it would split apart and vanish forever.

St. Paul Island has been a mariner's graveyard ever since ships began to visit the New World and is still a threat to navigation. Even today, with its modern lighthouses with flashes and horns that can be seen and heard for miles away, it remains a menacing sentinel of rock—a threat to the ships that sail the Strait.

Although the island is only about 3 mi. long by 1 mi. wide at its widest, it has a shoreline of about 12 mi. due to its intricate configuration of beaches, cliffs and chasms, many of which bear the names of the vessels they claimed. Indeed, St. Paul is a monument to the tragedies she has caused. Almost every headland, cove, and rock bears the name of a wreck—Norwegian Head, Sovereign Cove, Viceroy Cove, and Jessie Cove are of particular tragedies. For the first visitors to St. Paul, the shipwrecks were evidenced by numerous bits of wreckage and skeletons at the foot of isolated headlands. John Adams, an architect sent to St. Paul in 1830 to plan the first lighthouse wrote, "We minutely examined every cranny around the island in the ship's launch, and occasionally clambered on the rocks at the bases of the cliffs, but found no shelter. In all those bays and indentures, which are very numerous on the western side, we found remains of former wrecks piled up there high and dry—deals, staves, pieces of bulwark, planks of boats, etc., plainly indicative of past misfortune."

Later, in the 1800s, after shelters and lighthouses were built and manned, records show that the frequency and number of wrecks that occurred is astounding. In 1835, four vessels went down in one night and an expert on the island's history remarked, "it seems that an average of five vessels were lost on the island annually." Indeed, it is said that for every recorded wreck at St. Paul Island, there are two of unknown identity.

For those who live on the Atlantic coast or have visited its shores and witnessed a bad storm, the ferocity of the waves can never be forgotten. For them, the energy of the sea and the destruction it would have dealt to a ship driven on the rocks of St. Paul needs little imagination. This small but lethal island is hammered by thundering masses of ice from winter waters and lashed by the huge seas of summer storms. Ships caught up in this rage of nature had little chance of survival. The first superintendent appointed to St. Paul, John Campbell of Argyleshire, Scotland, wrote in his diary on January 18, 1844, that the billows of the Atlantic, "dash against the cliffs with such violence that the spray rises high against the side of the mountains perhaps to the height of 300 ft." It is hard to conceive of a vessel surviving against the rocks when caught in such swells.

LIKE THE COVES and headlands that have been named after shipwrecks, the discovery of a treasure passed on its name. Once, many years ago, one of the lighthouse keepers found a jug called a "crocan" containing 500 sovereigns. He discovered the crocan in a rocky crevice just above high tide. It was conjectured that a shipwrecked

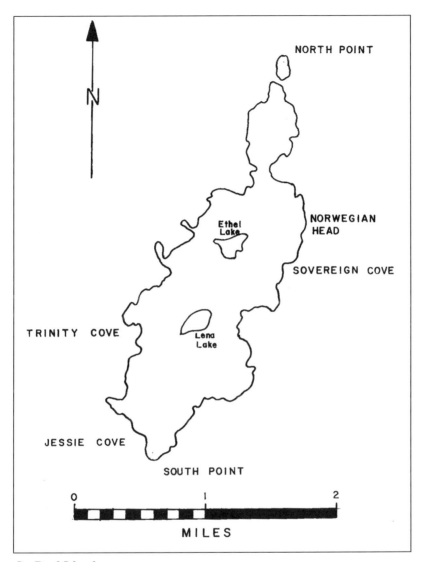

St. Paul Island.

sailor hid the treasure there but died before it could be retrieved. The place where this treasure was found received the name of Crocan Cove, and the hill of rock above the cove is called Crocan Mountain. Of all the places that have received names in memory of a wreck or a treasure, perhaps the best known is Jessie Cove. It is an unusual story of heartbreak and tragedy.

The barque *Jessie* sailed from Prince Edward Island on

December 21, 1824, with twenty-eight people aboard including her owner, Donald MacKay. As the barque sailed out of the Gulf of St. Lawrence and entered the waters of the Cabot Strait, she ran into a ferocious snowstorm and was blown toward St. Paul Island. On January 1, 1825, she was battered to pieces on the island's cliffs.

Some made it to shore where they fashioned a rough shelter from canvas and spars and built a large bonfire with the hope of signalling fishermen at Cape North, about 15 mi. away on the mainland of Cape Breton Island. But their fire failed to bring anyone to their rescue. Day after day they waited as hope of survival dwindled. Eventually they ran out of food, and one by one, died of starvation. Sometime in the early spring of 1825, fishermen went ashore on St. Paul, as was their annual routine, to search for valuables from wrecks of the previous seasons. They found the shelter and bodies of the *Jessie* disaster. The fishermen stripped the bodies of all their belongings, including a beautiful overcoat from one of the corpses. The coat belonged to Donald MacKay and had been made by his wife. In MacKay's clothing they found and removed 100 guineas.

When the *Jessie* failed to return on time, Donald MacKay's wife began to worry. Her consternation deepened as days turned to weeks, and weeks to months. Finally, she grievingly accepted that her husband was never to return. She was a seaman's widow.

One day, as she entered the village store, she was astonished to see her husband standing at the counter on the opposite side of the shop. She rushed over and discovered her mistake. The man was a stranger, but he was wearing her husband's coat. She recognized the garment that she had laboured so hard to create. The buttons on the sleeves were her handwork. There was no mistaking this article of clothing. "You have my husband's coat," she screamed and grabbed the man by the arm. "Where did you get it?"

The stranger tried to struggle from the woman's grip but before he could escape, she pulled open the garment and exposed the initials, D. M. which she had embroidered on the lining.

The stranger was restrained from leaving the shop by several of the villagers and after a barrage of questions, admitted to having taken it from a shipwreck shelter on St. Paul Island. He turned over the coat along with the one hundred guineas to Mrs. MacKay.

Donald MacKay's body was found and brought home along with the barque's captain. Most of the others were buried on St. Paul.

The loss of the *Jessie* and Mrs. MacKay's harrowing experience may have had some influence on the decision to protect ships from the cliffs of this dangerous island, for it was not long after that plans were made to build a lighthouse and shelters.

In the summer of 1832, the New Brunswick government sent workmen to build a shelter at Trinity Cove, on the west side of St. Paul Island. And, at the same time, three men with a Mr. MacKenzie in charge, were sent from Cape Breton to build a similar shelter on the opposite side. Although it seems incredible, given the narrow width of the island, it is said that neither party knew of the other's presence.

In midwinter of the following year, the *Great Britain*, bound from Quebec to Hull, England, tore her heart out on the jagged ledges near Trinity Cove. Four of the thirty men aboard reached shore. The rest were drowned.

Although the ship was destroyed near the New Brunswick shelter, only one man found it. He obviously became separated from the other three, who wandered across the snow-covered island. One man became separated from the trio and stumbled upon the Cape Breton station.

MacKenzie went in search of the two missing men. He retraced the tracks in the snow of the man who had reached his shelter and found two frozen bodies not far away. They had almost made it to safety. Continuing to follow footsteps in the snow, he crossed the island and ended up at the New Brunswick shelter. There, he found the fourth sailor who was in critical condition and died a short time later.

Finally, in 1837, John Campbell, of Argyleshire, Scotland, from whose diary I earlier quoted, was appointed superintendent of the island and his first job was to supervise the construction of lighthouses and a main station. Two lighthouses were constructed. One near the north end, called the Northeast Light and one near the south end, called the Southwest Light. But, despite the operation of lighthouses, ships continued to pile up onto the rocks of St. Paul, helping it to earn its well deserved nickname.

ONE OF THE EARLIEST treasure ships to founder at St. Paul may have been a Spanish galleon which was driven off course and crashed onto the rocks. Old Spanish gold coins were found on the sea bottom at the base of one of the cliffs. They were discovered by fishermen who for years brought them up with long poles. The men dipped the ends of the poles in pitch and probed around the sea bottom. The coins adhered to the pitch and large quantities were recovered in this manner. However, any heavy bars of silver and gold that may have been part of the ship's cargo could not be recovered by this method, and most of the galleon's treasure may still be at the base of the cliff. I have not read nor heard any report of its recovery.

One of the best known stories of wrecked ships bearing treasure is that of the *Royal Sovereign*. She was also one of the most disastrous wrecks to occur on the island's jagged rocks.

The *Royal Sovereign* was a British Royal Navy ship transporting troops back home to England following the War of 1812. There were about eight hundred passengers on board, including wives and children. The ship sailed out of the Gulf of St. Lawrence and made it safely through the strait, past St. Paul Island. She seemed to be well on her way for the open seas of the Atlantic when she was caught in a gale out of the southeast.

The *Royal Sovereign* was forced off course by strong currents and rough seas and driven onto the rocks of a cove that now bears her name, on the eastern side of St. Paul Island. Bodies soon washed up on shore and those who were fortunate to make it to shore could only watch as their ship was pounded to pieces by the raging sea.

A passing vessel picked up the survivors a few days later and landed them safely on the mainland. Of those who were drowned, some of the bodies drifted all the way to Sydney Harbour in Cape Breton, a distance of about 70 mi.

Silver coins were later found among the rocks near the site of the wreck and the story persists that the *Royal Sovereign* carried a consignment of Mexican silver coins. They were to be delivered to the British Royal Crown Mint for melting and re-coining. Some of the cannon balls and cannons from the wreck can still be seen today, strewn among the rocks near Sovereign Cove.

As for the better part of the *Royal Sovereign*'s treasure, it must still be out there and waiting for the adventurous treasure hunter, and so must the artifacts and treasures of numerous other wrecks that surround the rugged cliffs of St. Paul.

CHAPTER FIFTEEN

KIDD'S BOOTY

When most people think of pirates, the name "Captain William Kidd" comes first to mind. He is viewed as a bloodthirsty dog who went about burning villages to the ground, murdering men, women, and children and lopping off the heads of all those who opposed him. The name "Kidd" is virtually the symbol of piracy.

Kidd is also thought of as the grand master of buried treasure; renowned for burying doubloons, jewels, and pieces of eight. There is hardly a harbour, beach, or island from Newfoundland to Florida that hasn't at one time or another been the reputed burial ground of the infamous Captain Kidd.

It has been said that behind every legend is an event which has been so warped in the retelling that it no longer resembles the truth. This applies particularly to Kidd.

William Kidd was born in Greenock, Scotland, about 1645. He took to the sea at an early age and amassed a respectable fortune which allowed him to settle down in New York in 1691 where he married Sarah Oort, a well-to-do widow of a ship-master merchant.

In 1695, King William III was short of money and enlisted Kidd under the Great Seal of England to lead a privateering expedition to the Red Sea in an attempt to refill the royal coffers. The *Adventure Gallery* was selected for the mission, and Kidd sailed her to New York where he picked up additional crew and then struck out on his appointed task. Meanwhile, back in England, King William and the Whigs were forced to declare Kidd a pirate when the Tories exposed the use of the Great Seal of England on a personal privateering mission sponsored by the king. Orders for his arrest were issued.

In June 1699, Kidd anchored off Gardner's Island near the eastern end of Long Island Sound, while trying to have the warrant for his arrest rescinded. As a bargaining tool, he buried a load of gold and jewels on the island with the permission of its owner, John Gardner. Gardner was said to be a generous, upright, and agreeable man. He received payment from Kidd and gave him a receipt for the buried treasure.

Kidd's attempt to save his own life failed. He was arrested and thrown in prison on July 6, 1699, and hanged at Execution Dock, Wapping on May 23, 1701.

Between the time of his imprisonment and hanging, the Governor of New York, Lord Bellomont, dug up the cache on Gardener's Island. It was valued at £14,000.

FOR THREE CENTURIES, numerous searches for treasure believed to have been buried by Kidd have been made up and down the east coast of North America, the West Indies, Madagascar, and even on islands in the South China Sea. Much of this frantic searching is no doubt a result of two letters by Kidd, written while he was in prison, in which he baited the reader with claims of large fortunes that could be recovered—all obviously made in an attempt to avoid the hangman's noose. In the first letter, to the Earl of Orford, dated April 11, 1700, Kidd defended himself and advised of "£90,000, which is left in very good hands and I doubt not when I am clear of this trouble but to bring the same for England without any diminution." In the second letter, written to the Speaker of the House of Commons, dated May 12, 1701, while waiting execution, Kidd wrote, "in my late proceedings in the Indies, I have lodged goods and Treasure to the value of £100,000" and offers to go as a prisoner aboard a government vessel and lead the way to the horde.

The most popular "Kidd" legend concerns Oak Island, Nova Scotia. The majority of treasure hunters up to the mid-1900s, held to the belief that Kidd engineered the Money Pit.

According to legend, over three centuries ago an elderly man on his deathbed, in what was then known as the British Colony of New England, confessed to having been a member of Kidd's crew and swore that many years earlier he had helped Kidd and his men bury an enormous treasure on a secluded island east of Boston. The legend was widely spread and the early settlers brought the much-publicized tale to Nova Scotia. For a century following the alleged confession numerous searches were made, but the treasure was never found.

When the Money Pit on Oak Island was discovered in 1795, the early settlers believed that it was dug by pirates and elected Kidd. But the designer and builder of the complex system found on Oak Island had to have been a highly skilled and ingenious engineer. Kidd was not known to possess any appreciable engineering skills. Furthermore, engineers have estimated that it took an army of men at least two years to carry out the complex excavations. The writings by those who have researched Kidd's years as a privateer prove that there was insufficient time gaps in his voyages to visit Nova Scotia and construct the Oak Island complex. Also, Kidd commanded an unruly crew and lacked the manpower required for such an undertaking.

There are those who say there is proof that Kidd was active on the shores of Nova Scotia. This is their story. The settlers of a small Acadian fishing village awoke one morning to find what they perceived to be a pirate ship anchored in their little harbour. Before them stood a band of grim-faced men who they took to be buccaneers from the evil look in their eyes.

The ship had silently slipped into harbour during the night. The crew had rowed quietly ashore, and now in the wee hours of the morning, faced the frightened villagers.

The visitors obviously had a problem. Their vessel was without masts.

The captain of the vessel turned out to be a charismatic individual who immediately won over the villagers with his charm. He described being caught in a violent storm and how all the masts and rigging had been torn off the ship. He said that neither he nor his crew had any intentions of harming the people. Their only reason for being in the harbour was to repair their ship. Being a fishing village, he suspected that some of the men were handy at boatbuilding and repairs and hoped that they would be able to make masts and help refit the vessel. He promised that no harm would come to the people while the work was being done as long as the men of the village cooperated. Furthermore, the work must begin immediately and be carried out as quickly a possible. He stressed that although the men were not at liberty to refuse, he would pay generously for their labours.

The villagers worked long and hard while doing an excellent job of cutting and shaping new masts and making repairs. When the work was completed, the ship's skipper congenially called the villagers together and announced that he was none other than the infamous Captain William Kidd!

Kidd then offered payment for materials and labour but the villagers refused, knowing that the money was tainted with blood and might bring them misfortune and tragedy.

Kidd didn't force payment on the villagers, knowing that they were God-fearing souls. But, as he sailed away, he tossed bars of silver and gold overboard, expecting the villagers to pick them up after he was gone. The villagers, however, convinced that they were pirates' spoils, would not touch the ill-gotten gains.

Of all the numerous tales of Kidd and his treasure, "A Notable Lawsuit" by Franklin H. Head takes the prize. This is the slightly condensed story from *Dig for Pirate Treasure* by Robert I. Nesmith, taken from a document privately printed in 1897.

"The suit commenced some three years since by Mr. Frederick Law Olmsted against the various members of the Astor family in the New York Superior Court, attracted considerable attention at the time, both from the prominence of the parties to the litigation and the large amount claimed by Mr. Olmsted, something over $5 million. As the case has not come to a hearing, owing to the delays in the proceedings at law, the matter has, in a measure, passed from notice, scarcely anything connected with it having appeared in the public prints since the commencement of the action.

"Through the courtesy of Mr. Olmsted, I spent several days during the summer of 1895, as a guest at his summer residence on Deer Isle, which lies in Penobscot Bay, off the mouth of the Penobscot River, on the coast of Maine; and having heard quite in detail the history of the cause of action, which seemed to me a most forcible illustration of the maxim that truth is stranger than fiction, I take pleasure giving the story as told by Mr. Olmsted and the members of his family.

"An ancestor, several generations back, of Mr. Olmsted, whose name was Cotton Mather Olmsted, was an Indian trader, and spent a part of each year from 1696 to 1705, in what is now the State of Maine. His treatment of the Indians was always fair and honourable, whereby he won their confidence and esteem. Winnepesaukee, then the head sachem of the Penobscot tribe, was at one time severely wounded by a bear, and Mr. Olmsted having cared for him, dressed his wounds, and aided greatly in his recovery. The chief, as a token of gratitude, presented to him the Deer Isle before named, a portion of which has ever since remained in the possession of his descendants, and is now the property and summer home of Mr. Frederic Law Olmsted. The original deed of gift, written on a piece of birch-bark, and bearing the date January 24, 1699, is still in the possession of Mr. Olmsted, and after the independence of the United Sates was acknowledged, the validity of the transfer was recognized and affirmed, and a formal patent issued by the Secretary of the Treasury during the second term of President Washington's administration.

"Upon the rocky shore near the residence of Mr. Olmsted, and at the extreme south end of the island is a cave, the opening of which is upon the sea. The cave is about 10 ft. wide and high, of irregular shape, and extends back into the rock formation some 25 ft. It has evidently been excavated by the ceaseless action of the waves upon a portion of the rock somewhat softer than its surroundings. At high tide the entire cave is under water, but at low tide it can be entered dry-shod being entirely above the sea-level. The bottom of the cave is covered with coarse sand, 5 or 6 in. deep, below which is a compact bed of hard blue clay. At low tide the cave is often visited by the family of Mr. Olmsted, and the other residents of the island. In 1892, Mr. Olmsted observed upon the rock at the inner end of the cave some marks or indentations, something in the form of a rude cross, which seemed to him possibly of artificial origin. If so, it was of ancient date, as its edges were not well defined—were rounded and worn, as by the action of the waves and ice. Still, it appeared more regular in form than the other markings upon the walls of the cave, and Mr. Olmsted one day suggested to his family, when in the cave, that as stories of Captain Kidd's buried treasures had sometimes located such treasures upon the Maine coast, they should dig at the place below the cross for such hidden wealth. Purely as a matter of sport, the excavation was commenced: the sand was cleared away, and, to their surprise, a rectangular hole in the clay was discovered, about 15 by 30 in. on the surface and about 15 in. deep. This was filled with sand, and upon the sand being carefully removed, there was plainly to be seen upon the bottom of the hole the marks of a row of bolt heads some 3 or 4 in. apart, and extending around the bottom about 1 in. from its edge. The appearance was precisely as if an iron box heavily bolted at its joints had been buried in the compact clay for a period long enough to have left a perfect impress of itself in the clay, and after its removal, the excavation having been filled with sand, the impression had been perfectly preserved. After a perfect facsimile of the bottom of the hole had been taken in plaster of Paris, the excavation was again filled with sand. The clay was so hard that the taking of the cast did not mar its surface. The bottom of the hole and such portions of the sides as had not been marred by the removal of the box were heavily coated with iron-rust, so that everything indicated the former presence of an iron box which remained buried in the clay long enough at least to become thoroughly rusted on its surface and firmly embedded in the clay matrix. As there were various legends relative to the presence of Captain Kidd upon the Maine coast, the discovery of the excavation was sufficient to awaken eager interest in the question of the iron box and the person who carried it away.

"About the year 1801 a French-Canadian named Jacques Cartier, who was one of the employees of John Jacob Astor in his fur trade, and who had for several winters traded with the Indians and hunters along the upper waters of the Penobscot River, returned from New York, where he had been to deliver the season's collection of furs, and expressed a desire to purchase from Oliver Cromwell Olmsted, who was then the owner, by inheritance, of Deer Isle, either the whole island or the south end, where the cave before described was located. Mr. Olmsted refused both requests, but finally sold him a few acres near the center of the island, where he built a log house and lived for many years with an Indian wife, hunting and fishing occasionally as a diversion, but giving up entirely his former method of gaining a livelihood. This trader had for several years previous to 1801 camped upon the south end of Deer Isle when collecting his furs, passing up the Penobscot River and its tributaries in a small canoe, and storing his furs in a hut at his camping-place until the end of his season, when he sailed with his little cargo for New York. He had always seemed extremely poor, having but a meager salary from Mr. Astor, but when he purchased a portion of the island he seemed to have an abundance of money, sufficient in fact to meet his wants for many years. Occasionally, when under the influence of whiskey, he would speak vaguely of some sudden good fortune which had befallen him, but when sober he always denied ever having made the statement, and seemed much disturbed when asked about the source of his wealth, which led to various suspicions among the few inhabitants of the island as to the honesty of his methods in acquiring it. These suspicions ultimately became so pointed that he suddenly disappeared from the island and never returned. On searching his cabin some fragments of papers were found, torn and partially burned, so that no connected meaning could be determined from them. On one fragment was the signature of John Jacob Astor, and on another, in the same handwriting, the words: 'absolute secrecy must be observed because ...' These fragments were preserved, however, and are now in the possession of Mr. Frederick Law Olmsted. From the story of the trader and from the fragmentary papers, Mr. Olmsted fancied that there might be some connection between the mysterious box and the newly acquired wealth of the trader, and that the secret, if there was one, was shared by Mr. Astor. As the trader for many years previous to his sudden good fortune had camped upon the end of the island immediately adjoining the cave, it might readily be conceived that a heavy storm had washed the sand away so as to make the top of the box visible, and that he had found and taken it with him to New York to Mr. Astor, with his boatload of furs. His desire to purchase this particular location in the island harmonized with this suggestion.

"Various questions presented themselves regarding this theory. Had the box contained the long-lost treasure of Captain Kidd? If so, to whom did the box and its contents belong? Mr. William M. Evarts, to whom Mr. Olmsted applied for an opinion as to the legal phase of this question, after careful examination of the evidence, gave his views, in substance as follows:

1. That Captain Kidd, in the year 1700, had acquired, by pillage, vast treasures of gold and gems, which he had somewhere concealed prior to his execution in 1701.

2. That if such treasure was concealed upon Deer island, that island was the absolute property, at that time, of Cotton Mather Olmsted; for while the record title to the island bore date in President Washington's administration in 1794, yet this, as appeared by its tenor, was in affirmation of the title made in 1699, when the island was given to Cotton Mather

Olmsted by the Indian chief, Winnepesaukee, and established the ownership of the island in Mr. Olmsted when the box, if concealed by Captain Kidd, was buried, and that Frederick Law Olmsted, by inheritance and purchase, had acquired all the rights originally held by his ancestor in that part of the island where the treasure was concealed.

3. That, as owner of such real estate, the treasure would belong to him, as affixed to the land, as against the whole world, except possibly the lineal descendants of Captain Kidd, if any there were.

"Mr. Olmsted learned that, in his early life, Mr. Astor kept for many years his first and only bank account with the Manhattan Bank, and as the books of the bank are all preserved, he was enabled, by a plausible pretext, to secure an examination of Mr. Astor's financial transactions from the beginning. His idea, in this search, was to learn if Mr. Astor's fortune had increased at the same time as that of the French-Canadian. The business of both Mr. Astor and the bank was small in those early days, and the entries of the customers' accounts were much more in detail than in our time, when, as a rule, only amounts are recorded. The account commenced in 1798, being one of the first accounts opened after the picturesque organization of the bank of Aaron Burr, and for several years the total deposits for an entire year did not exceed $4,000. He shipped some of his furs abroad, and others were sold to dealers and manufacturers, and whenever he drew on a customer with a bill of lading, the books of the bank show virtually the whole transaction. Entries like the following are of frequent occurrence:

Cr. J. J. Astor, $33. proceeds draft for sale of 40 Muskrat, 4 Bear, 3 Deer and 12 Mink Skins.
Credit John J. Astor $49.50, proceeds of draft for sale of 400 Skunk Skins.
Cr. John Jacob Astor $131. proceeds of draft on London for 26 pounds/10 shillings for sale 87 Otter Skins, 46 Mink and 30 Beaver Pelts.

"Each year showed a modest increase in the volume of business of the thrifty furrier, but the aggregates were only moderate until the year 1801, being the same year the Canadian trader bought of Mr. Olmsted a portion of Deer Island, when the volume of bank transactions reached, for the

time, enormous dimensions, springing from an aggregate for
the year 1799 of $4,011 to over $500,000 for the year 1801.
Among the entries in the latter year are two of the same date
for cheques to Jacques Cartier, the French-Canadian: one of
$133.50, drawn 'In settlement fur account,' and one for
$5,000, 'In settlement to date.' Inasmuch as in each previous
year the aggregate fur transactions with Mr. Cartier had never
exceeded $500, the entry of $5,000 seemed inexplicable on
any ordinary grounds.

"The enormous growth of Mr. Astor's own transactions
also seemed equally mysterious. Mr. Astor had evidently
visited England in the year 1801, as the bank entries are filled
with credits to him of drafts remitted by him from Roderick
Streeter, varying from £10,000 to £40,000, and aggregating,
during the year, nearly $495,000. Credits of the same Streeter
drafts are made also during the two following years to the
amount of over $800,000 more, or a total of over $1,300,000,
when the Streeter remittances abruptly cease. Edwin W.
Streeter of London is at the present time one of the largest
dealers in precious stones in the world, and as in England the
same business is often continued in a family for many generations, it occurred to Mr. Frederick Law Olmsted, who, from
the facts already given, had become greatly interested in
following the matter to conclusion, that the Streeter who had
made the vast remittances to Mr. Astor might be an ancestor
of the present London merchant. An inquiry by mail
developed the fact that the present Mr. Streeter was a great-
grandson of Roderick Streeter, and that the business had been
continued in the family for five generations. Mr. Olmsted
thereupon sent a confidential agent to London, who
succeeded in getting access to the books of the Streeter firm
for the years 1798 to 1802, inclusive. Here was found a
detailed statement of the transactions with Mr. Astor. The
first item was for £40,000 entered as 'Advances on ancient
French and Spanish Gold Coins' deposited by Mr. Astor, and
later another £4,213 /8 shillings for 'Balance due for the
French and Spanish gold coins.' All other entries were for the
sale of precious stones, mostly diamonds, rubies and pearls,
which in all, with the sums paid for the French and Spanish
gold, reached the enormous aggregate heretofore given.
Certain of the gems were purchased outright by Mr. Streeter

and others were sold by him, as a broker, for the account of Mr. Astor, and the proceeds duly remitted during the years 1801–1802. The whole account corresponded exactly, item for item, with the various entries of Streeter remittances shown on the books of the Manhattan Bank.

"The facts gathered thus far enabled Mr. Olmsted to formulate a theory in substance as follows: That Jacques Cartier had found the box containing the buried treasures of Captain Kidd; that he had taken it to New York and delivered it to Mr. Astor; that Mr. Astor had bought the contents of the box, or his interest in them, for the cheque of $5,000; that he had taken the contents to England, and had, from their sale, realized the vast sums paid him by Mr. Streeter. Many links in the chain of evidence, however, were still missing, and a great point would be gained if the mysterious box could be traced to the custody of Mr. Astor. It seemed reasonable that the box, if ever in the possession of Mr. Astor, and if its contents were of such great value, would be retained by him with scrupulous care, and that, if he had imparted the secret to his children, it would still be in their possession. If not, it might have been sold and lost sight of, as a piece of worthless scrap-iron, after the death of the first Mr. Astor. Mr. Olmsted learned that the last house in which the original John Jacob Astor had lived had been torn down in the year 1893, to be replaced by a superb modern building, and that the old building had been sold to a well-known house wrecking firm for an insignificant sum, as the material was worth but little above the cost of tearing down and removal. In the hope that the rusty box had been sold with other rubbish about the premises, Mr. Olmsted inserted the following advertisement in the *New York Tribune.*

> A rusty iron box, strongly made and bolted, was by mistake sold in 1893 to a dealer in junk, supposedly in New York or Brooklyn. The dimensions were 15 x 30 x 15 in. A person, for sentimental reasons, wishes to reclaim this box, and will pay to its present owner for the same several times its value as scrap-iron. Address F.L. Box 74, N.Y. Tribune.

"Within a few days, Mr. Olmsted received a letter from Mr. Bronson B. Tuttle of Naugatuck, Connecticut, an iron manufacturer, stating that, in a car of scrap-iron bought by him from Melchisedec Jacobs of Brooklyn, was an iron box answering the description given in the *Tribune*; that if it was of any value to the advertiser, it would be forwarded on receipt of eighty cents, which was its cost to him at $11 per ton, the price paid for a carload of scrap. Mr. Olmsted at once procured the box and shipped it to Deer Island, where the bolts upon its bottom and the box itself, were found to fit perfectly the print in the clay bottom of the cave. The plaster cast of the bottom of the cavity, taken when it was discovered, matched the bottom of the box as perfectly as ever a casting fitted the mold in which it was made. Every particularity in the shape of a bolt head, every hammer-mark made in riveting the bolts, as shown in the clay, was reproduced in the iron box. There was no possible question that the box was the identical one which had been long before buried in the cave. On the top of the box, too, was distinguishable despite the heavy coating of rust, in rude and irregularly formed characters, as if made by strokes of a cold chisel or some similar tool, the letters W.K., the initials of the veritable and eminent pirate, Captain William Kid."

Olmsted's agent researched Kidd's career and among the stories of his privateering, arrest and execution passed along the information that Kidd's wife had only been allowed to see him for a half hour after the pronouncement of his sentence but "They [Kidd and his wife] held a whispered conference, and at its close he was seen to hand her a card, upon which he had written the figures 44106818." The guards took the card away from Kidd's wife and it became preserved "among the proceedings of the trial." Mrs. Kidd could never be induced to reveal the meaning of the digits. Olmsted acquired a photographed copy and the answer came quite unexpectedly. It came in the summer of 1894 when a Professor David P. Todd, astronomer of Amherst College, was visiting the Olmsted family at Deer Island. "He [Professor Todd] one day amused himself by calculating the latitude and longitude of the home, near the cave, and gave the results to Miss Marion Olmsted. As she was entering the results in her journal, she was struck by the fact that the figures for the latitude, 44° and 10′, were the same as the first four figures on the card, 4410, and that the other four figures, 6818, were almost the exact longitude west from Greenwich, which was 68° and 13′, a difference easily accounted for by a moderate variation in Capt. Kidd's chronometer. The latitude, taken by observation of the pole-star, was absolutely accurate."

Records of Captain Kidd's trial showed that there were no descendants to make "any claim upon the treasure," so at this point it seemed that the only evidence that was now needed was to "show that some of the money or gems sold by him [Astor] had been actually seized by Captain Kidd." That evidence became possible through the Streeter correspondence.

The story word for word says, "It appears that, in the year 1700, Lord and Lady Dunmore were returning to England from India, when the vessel upon which they had taken passage was fired upon and captured by Capt. Kidd. His first order was that every person on board should walk the plank into the sea, but several ladies who were passengers pleaded so earnestly for their lives, that Kidd finally decided to plunder the cargo and passengers and let the vessel proceed on her voyage. The ladies were compelled, on peril of their lives, to surrender all their jewelry, and among the articles taken from Lady Dunmore was a pair of superb pearl bracelets, the pearls being set in a somewhat peculiar fashion. Another pair, an exact duplicate of those possessed by Lady Dunmore, had been purchased by Lord Dunmore as a wedding gift for his sister, and the story of the two pairs of bracelets and the loss of Lady Dunmore's pearls, which were of great value, and of her pleading for her life to Capt. Kidd, is a matter of history, as well as one of the cherished family traditions. In 1801, Roderick Streeter writes to Mr. Astor that the then Lady Dunmore, in looking over some gems which he was offering her, had seen a pair of exquisite pearl bracelets which were a part of the Astor consignment, and had at once recognized them as the identical pair taken by Kidd nearly one hundred years before. She returned the following day, with the family solicitor, bringing the duplicate bracelets; told and verified the story of the loss of one pair by Lady Dunmore; compared the two pairs, showing their almost perfect identity, showing certain private marks upon each, and demonstrating beyond question that the pearls offered by Mr. Streeter were the identical gems seized by Captain Kidd. The solicitor demanded their surrender to Lady Dunmore on the ground that, having been stolen, no property in them could pass even to an innocent purchaser. Mr. Streeter then stated that he had asked for delay until he could communicate with the owner of the gems, and asked Mr. Astor for instructions. Mr. Astor replied, authorizing the delivery of the bracelets to Lady Dunmore, and asking Mr. Streeter to assure her that the supposed owner was guiltless of wrong in the matter, and was an entirely innocent holder. He repeated the caution, given also in sundry other letters, that on no account was the ownership of the gems sold by Mr. Streeter to be revealed. They were to be sold as the property of Streeter, acquired in the regular course of business. Lady Dunmore afterward sat to Sir Thomas Lawrence for her portrait, and was painted wearing upon her arms the pearl bracelets thus curiously reclaimed. This portrait is considered one of the masterpieces of Lawrence and is now in the collection of Mr. Hall McCormick of Chicago."

Olmsted formulated the evidence and called upon the Astor descendants who had vastly benefited and demanded $1,300,000 plus interest. The descendants refused. Because Astral had expended over $700,000 of the $1,300,000 he had received from the Streeter remittances in the purchase of New York real estate, all of which was still in the Astor family, Olmsted then demanded that "the Astor family should convey to him all the real estate in New York City purchased by their ancestor with the money received from Streeter, with the accrued rents and profits from the date of purchase." This demand was also refused.

We are told that the matter finally went to court but we are not informed of the outcome.

According to Edward Rowe Snow who tells the story in his book *Ghosts, Gales and Gold*, Frederick Law Olmsted was one of the summer visitors to Deer Island in the 1890s. There he became acquainted with Franklin H. Head of Chicago. Head wrote "A Notable Lawsuit" to amuse the Olmsted family and, Robert Nesmith writes, "This tale was written for amusement in 1894." It is just an amusing hoax. However, true or false, it probably is as true as most Captain Kidd tales.

If nothing of worth has come from the life of Captain William Kidd, at least he was the catalyst behind the Deer Island story and hundreds of others. In a subtle way, the story exonerates Kidd to some extent. Although the yarn is uncannily believable it is possibly as phony as the public perception of Kidd—the most wronged man in marine history.

CHAPTER SIXTEEN

ACADIAN GOLD

The first settlers of Nova Scotia (then called Acadia) were the French. These hardy souls who held the name of Acadians, landed in 1605 and established Canada's first settlement at Port Royal on the Bay of Fundy side of the province, near the mouth of the Annapolis River.

France was intent on strengthening her political and economic position in the New World through colonization and in 1630 added the settlement of LaHave to the Atlantic coast of Nova Scotia. Although LaHave offered an excellent base for a fishing industry because of its fine harbour and sheltered inlets, it had a lot to be desired as an agricultural area. As the new settlers had to farm as well as fish to survive, they soon moved to the Port Royal region.

The many tidal marshlands of the Annapolis Basin and along the Annapolis River were ideal for farming. The Acadians built dykes to hold back the high Fundy tides and reclaimed large areas of fertile soil. Acadian settlements spread to similar marshlands of the Bay of Fundy and over the years the population center gradually shifted away from Port Royal. By 1720 the majority of Acadians inhabited the Minas Basin region. Between 1748 and 1750, the population of Port Royal was only 1,750 to that of 5,000 in the Minas Basin region.

For nearly 150 years, the Acadians farmed the fertile marshlands and enjoyed a peaceful lifestyle strengthened by a strong sense of religion. They lived on friendly terms with the Mi'kmaq and established a strong trading link with New England. Although the British and French were frequently waging war, the Acadians avoided taking sides and had no strong ties with either country. Sadly, the harmonious lives of the Acadians was destined to end. When France lost the War of the Spanish Succession, she was forced to sign the Treaty of Utrecht in 1713 which gave mainland Nova Scotia to the British and the islands of Prince Edward, Cape Breton, St. Pierre and Miquelon to the French. Consequently, to protect what remained, the French began construction of the huge fortress of Louisbourg which took almost thirty years to build, at a cost of millions of dollars. Once built, Louisbourg was considered a serious threat by the British as were the 10,000 or more Acadians living on the British Nova Scotia peninsula. It was unusual to have a British colony populated by French settlers.

Following the 1713 Treaty of Utrecht, Acadian loyalty to the British crown became a contentious issue for English colonial and military officials. The loyalty of the Acadians was always doubted by the British and the alliance of the Mi'kmaq with the Acadians was a serious source of concern.

The Treaty of Utrecht had left the western boundary that now separates Nova Scotia from New Brunswick, on the Isthmus of Chignecto, ambiguous and undefined. Here lies the Chignecto marshlands of the Missaguash River, and here on the marshlands, the Acadians had been established for almost one hundred years. So, this was a very sensitive area. The French claimed the region west of the Missaguash River and in 1750, the British built Fort Lawrence, near present-day Amherst, on the east bank of the river. The next year, the French built Fort Beauséjour on the opposite side of the river bank. On the Missaguash River, the two super-powers were poised opposite each other as if for war.

The Treaty of Utrecht of 1713 stipulated that the Acadians could remain on their own lands with the proviso that they swear allegiance to the king of England. They could practice their religion but would have no say in the manner in which they were governed. They could not vote, join the army or hold public office. However, the Acadian parish priests were supplied by France and answered to the Bishop of Quebec and operated outside the British sphere of influence.

The Acadians were reluctant to swear an oath of allegiance to the monarch of Britain if it meant taking up arms against their fellow Frenchmen or the Mi'kmaq during a war. Consequently, the British authorities promised them that they would not have to fight the French or the Mi'kmaq, and by the end of the 1720s the majority of Acadians had signed the oath. The promise was sometimes written in the margin of the oath document or, as illiteracy was very high among the Acadians, the promise was sometimes simply given verbally.

In December 1729, Governor Philipps administered the oath to men over fifteen years of age. And although he promised that they would not be asked to fight the French or Mi'kmaq, he did not inform his superiors in Britain of the promise. Although the Acadians indicated a desire to walk the line of neutrality, Governor William Shirley of Massachusetts and Lieutenant-Governor Charles Lawrence of Nova Scotia were unconvinced—perhaps in part due to Philipps's omission. As hostilities between the French and British grew, British authorities became increasingly concerned over the Acadian's neutrality.

On June 4, 1755, 2,300 British troops attacked Fort Beauséjour on the Missaguash River. The Acadians defended their fort and thus violated their oath of neutrality.

Following the siege of Fort Beauséjour, New England troops that had been sent by Governor Shirley of Massachusetts to assist in the capture of Fort Beauséjour, were ordered to seize firearms and ammunition from the Acadians. Later, all Acadians in Nova Scotia were ordered to surrender their firearms. Subsequently, delegates from Acadian settlements arrived in Halifax, requesting the return of their guns. When they arrived, they were ordered to sign an unconditional oath of allegiance, an oath without a promise that they would not be required to bear arms against the French or the Mi'kmaq. They refused to sign and were thrown into prison on George's Island in Halifax Harbour.

In July 1755, Governor Lawrence ordered the Acadians to send a delegation to Halifax to settle the question of unconditional allegiance to the British Crown. When they arrived, they too were ordered to sign an unconditional oath. Like those delegates before them, they refused and were thrown into prison.

On July 28, 1755, Governor Lawrence and his council decided to remove all "French Inhabitants" from the colony of Nova Scotia.

The Expulsion began on August 11, 1755, at Fort Beauséjour (renamed Fort Cumberland). One month later the Expulsion began at Grand Pré, in the Minas Basin region. At Fort Beauséjour, the inhabitants were rounded up, imprisoned in the fort, and shipped off to British colonies on the east coast. At Grand Pré, the male inhabitants were ordered to assemble in the church on September 5 at three o'clock in the afternoon. As in other settlements, the assembled men were told that "their lands, their homes, and their livestock would be confiscated and that they and their families would be transported out of the province."

In the most traumatic event of Nova Scotian history, an estimated 6,000 Acadians were deported from the Nova Scotia peninsula in 1755. Between October and November of that year, about 2,200 were expelled from the Grand Pré area of the Minas Basin. On deportation, the British torched their homes and butchered their cattle.

Many Acadians perished on board the transport ships, while the survivors were allotted to American colonies from Massachusetts to South Carolina. Hundreds of Acadians made their way back to Nova Scotia but many families were not able to resettle on their ancestral lands. By the mid-1760s, all the Acadian farmlands of the Minas Basin and Annapolis Valley regions had been reoccupied by Protestant colonists from New England, called the "Planters."

According to tradition, the Acadians buried their valuables before being expelled with the intent of later returning for them. While the men were being rounded up and taken into captivity, the women and children are said to have stashed gold and silver coins and precious belongings into ceramic jugs and copper pots and buried them as quickly and as best they could.

From the descendants of the New England Planters, we hear tales of people of Acadian descent returning and searching for lost treasure. Ellis Gertridge, of the Gaspereau Valley, a former Acadian settlement in the Minas Basin region, told me one such story. Gertridge, in his seventies, recalls hearing of a gentlemen returning about fifty or sixty years ago and searching for a cache along the banks of the Gaspereau River. The man searched for a few days and then disappeared. Later, a hole was found in the ground in the vicinity of the search. In the hole was the imprint of a ceramic jug that had been removed.

Another story tells of a farmhand who mysteriously disappeared while ploughing a field beside the Gaspereau River. When the land owner who hired the worker dropped by to inspect work in progress, he found the horse and plow deserted. The farmhand was nowhere in site and never was heard from or seen again. Looking about the plowed field, the owner discovered a hole in the ground where the worker had dug out something. It was suspected that the plow had struck a cache and that the worker had made off with a horde of gold.

Of the stories handed down about Acadians who returned for their buried treasures, various versions of one particular tale prevails.

It involves a mother and her little girl. They arrived at a New England Planter's farmhouse about fifty years after the Expulsion of the Acadians and requested permission to dig for something that their ancestors had left behind. The owners consented and left the mother and child to the task while they went about their own business of the day. At the end of the day, the owners went looking for the mother and little girl but they had vanished. The next day the

Some senior residents of Gaspereau hold to the tradition that Acadian treasure caches were buried on or near the mud banks of the river.

owners looked around again and found an old well had been uncovered in a remote corner of their farm. They concluded that a treasure had been concealed in the well by an Acadian family prior to deportation.

David Christianson, Curator and Archaeologist of the Nova Scotia Museum, recalls hearing a similar version of this tale. "It would be interesting to collect a number of these stories and put them together for similarities," he told me. Christianson has a good point. With several stories that seem to have a common base, one might be able to pick out similar elements. With pieces of the tale that match, one might be able to reconstruct the original event. From that reconstruction, it is not inconceivable that the treasure site and even the original habitation might be discovered.

Another story from folklore tells of the Acadians gathering together before the deportation and melting down all their gold into the shape of a church bell and burying it. They may have chosen a well to eliminate the task of digging a new hole. The bell could have been lowered to the bottom of the well shaft and remained concealed under water. They may have covered the well by backfilling it with soil. Any trace of the well may have been lost to the elements over

The Gaspereau River Valley—site of early Acadian settlement and reputed site of buried treasure caches.

the years. The settlers had anticipated the Expulsion and conducted this collective act with the expectation of returning for the treasure at a safer time. What they may not have anticipated, was the re-settling of the lands by the British immediately following the Expulsion. The legend seems worthy of mention because the Acadians were a people who worked collectively. They teamed together to build and maintain their massive system of dykes from which they reclaimed thousands of acres of fertile marshland. And, whenever a young couple began a home, the whole village turned out to clear land and build a house for them. So a collective concealment of treasure has a ring of reality. But why pour the melted gold into the shape of a church bell? Why not ingots? Could the bell have been a church bell used as a container to hold the melted gold or the mold upon which the melted gold was poured? Perhaps, after years of retelling the tale, the mold or container became a gold bell.

The gold bell is thought to have been buried on land now owned by Sainte-Famille Wines Limited, a small family-owned vineyard and winery in Falmouth. The Sainte-Famille property is located on an original Acadian village site known as "La Paroisse Sainte Famille De Pisiguit."

The tales of hidden Acadian treasures hold some credibility for me because I believe that the Acadians would not have trusted the British to the extent of taking anything as valuable as gold and silver with them. It seems logical that they did, indeed, bury treasures. But where? With all the agriculture over the years, why don't we hear more stories of caches having been uncovered? Perhaps the answer lies in the communal work habits of the Acadians which is signified in the legend of the gold bell. As it was the nature of the Acadians to combine their efforts, is it likely that each householder made an individual deposit? Or is it more likely that the women and children of a village gathered together their little treasures and made a communal deposit—perhaps a deposit assisted by one or more of the men who avoided congregating with his brothers at the village church?

Not all the stories of buried Acadian treasure belong to tradition. The first English settlers following the Expulsion of the Acadians, held as a well-known fact that a French warship carrying a cargo of treasure escaped from Louisbourg during the siege.[1] She may have tried to strike out for France but whatever may have been her destination, she was detected by the British and chased into Caribou Harbour on the Northumberland Strait, the body of water separating Nova Scotia from Prince Edward Island.

There was only one narrow entrance to the harbour at that time (the geological changes that have created a second entrance are discussed in Chapter Twelve) and the British didn't follow their prey in. They may have made the decision not to pursue beyond the harbour inlet due to lack of navigational knowledge of the waters. The French vessel didn't reappear and after some half-hearted rowboat reconnaissance, the British concluded that she had gone ashore in some creek for there was no sign of her in the harbour. They abandoned the hunt.

Not long after the arrival of the first British settlers, Dr. John Harris and an elder brother, Matthew, from New England who settled in the now present town of Pictou around 1767 decided to search for the war vessel and her treasure. They set out in log canoes and paddled out of Pictou Harbour and around the coast to Caribou Harbour. Inside the harbour, they began a search for a creek where the treasure ship was thought to have landed. They travelled up the south shore of the harbour until they reached the mouth of the Caribou River. Was this the creek? They thought it possible and paddled up the river to where it forks from the Big and Little Caribou Rivers. Here, they decided that each would take a separate route. The doctor would go up the Big Caribou and his brother would follow up the Little Caribou which branches off at about right angles to the main stream. Each man carried a horn which he would blow to alert the other if either found the ship.

On going around a point of land formed by the junction of the rivers, Matthew Harris hadn't travelled far when he came upon a little cove. There, snugly beached, was the treasure ship. About a century later, in *A History of the County of Pictou*, Nova Scotia, Rev. George Patterson writes, "The channel of the river is deep, but somewhat crooked, and those on board must have been thoroughly acquainted with it to have brought her here, and to have selected this spot to run her ashore. So completely concealed was she by the bend in the shore and intervening woods, that Harris was within 10 yd. before she was seen."

On hearing his brother's horn, Dr. Harris hurried back down the Big River, rounded the point and shared Matthew's delight of discovery. The two men examined their prize. She was a neat and trim vessel with all her rigging intact. She had been armed, but the cannon was missing and it was presumed that it had been thrown overboard. (Probably during the chase to lighten the ship and increase the speed.)

From the treasure ship's beached position, the brothers decided that she could be salvaged as there would be little difficulty in getting her off and afloat. They planned to quickly return with men and equipment to do the job and told their families and friends of their discovery. But when they returned they found the vessel burned to the water's edge. She has been torched by the Indians who had been left in charge of the vessel with instructions not to touch her but to burn her at once if the English discovered her.

Patterson doesn't say if there was any treasure on board the ship when she was discovered nor does he indicate that it was removed by the Indians. However, in the history, he writes, "It is certain that vessels escaped from Louisbourg with treasure during the siege, and there is strong reason to believe that this had contained valuables, which those on board, when they abandoned her, could not carry away and conceal." So, it appears that the treasure was removed by the French when they beached the vessel. The historical account goes on to suggest that the treasure may have been recovered. One evening, about the year 1802, a ship dropped anchor off the inlet of Caribou Harbour, and a boat manned by an able crew was spotted going up the Big Caribou River. No one saw the boat return but the ship pulled anchor early the next morning and sailed away. A short time later, some of the local people going up the river noticed a place at the head of the tide where work had been carried out. A shallow hole, perhaps 4 ft. deep and between 4 and 6 ft. square had been dug in the ground. The hole had hand-spokes (grips or handholds fixed along the rim of a ship's steering wheel) positioned in a way that suggested to the settlers that a chest or something like one had been pried out from the bottom of the hole. The hole was some distance from the beached treasure ship and on the main branch of the river. On examining the area, the searchers found trees bearing marks pointing to the hole.

About 1820, a resident of Caribou Island, James A. Harris, son of Dr. Harris's brother Matthew, pointed out to his son James the keel of the treasure ship and some of the timbers which were still standing. Checking with an axe, they discovered that the wood was American white oak. Rev. Patterson remarked, "Probably some remains of her might yet be found in the mud."

Of other Acadian treasures, Rev. Patterson notes that there had been other stories of the French burying money "in the hurry of leaving and the expectation of returning" and tells the story of a settler reputedly finding a large sum of money. He writes, "A son of the settler referred to, told a gentleman who reported the case to me, that it was true—that he and his sister, both then children, first found the money under a stump, that it consisted entirely of old coins, strange to him, but whether French or not he did not know; that they told their father of it, who gathered them, but gave them none of it. The story commonly received is that he took it to his merchant who shipped it to England, both agreeing to say nothing about the matter lest government should claim the amount. The merchant in the meantime supplied the settler abundantly with articles for his family, but afterward failed, so that they received little more for their find. Other facts that we have, give probability to the story."

The early English settlers of Pictou County found traces of Acadian settlements, the largest being at Merigomish Harbour on what was then referred to as the big island of Merigomish. There they found the foundations of seven or eight dwellings and a variety of articles were picked up such as shovels, knives, spoons, crockery and a few "coins."

In 1873, an old man told Rev. Patterson that in his boyhood he had found beads and other articles among the ruins of old Acadian dwelling houses at the upper part of Little Harbour. He also told Patterson that "some of the first settlers had told him that they had found a brass kettle under almost every chimney."

Rev. Patterson writes that although the Acadians of Pictou County are viewed as having been principally engaged in fishing, the tradition is that the shores of Caribou Harbour, where evidence of Acadian settlement was found, "abounded with large oak, which they cut and shipped to Louisbourg, where it was largely used in the construction of the city, and probably also in shipbuilding."

A number of years prior to the original publication of Rev. Patterson's history in 1877, a Charles McGee, of Merigomish, stayed at the house of a Mr. Petitpas as he passed Big Tracadie, while on his way up the coast from the Strait of Canso. During the course of the evening conversation, he learned that Mr. Petipas's father had been one of the Acadian settlers of Merigomish. Mr. Petipas's mother, who was very old and infirm but took part in the conversation, said that if she were able to go to the place, "she could yet show them where she had buried a large brass kettle, containing a number of household articles."

There are those who say that the Acadians had little wealth to bury but that contention draws a bit of comment. While millions of dollars were being pumped into Louisbourg for its construction and operation, the Acadians exported grains and livestock to Louisbourg in exchange for silver and gold coins which were used in a black market trade with New England. The Acadians, not being totally self-sufficient, imported such things as metal tools and millstones from New England. So there was a cash flow, as we now call it, and it is reasonable to believe that some of the more wealthy Acadian families must have had money to conceal prior to their expulsion. And, as noted in Patterson's history, tradition has it that the Acadians of Pictou provided oak wood to Louisbourg for construction work on the fortress and the building of ships.

Generally, the Acadians were in the trading business. They traded extensively with Louisbourg, the Anglo-American colonies, England, and France. They traded raw materials like wheat, barley, furs, and cattle for a wide range of goods such as ceramics, cloth, spices, tools, household utensils, harrows, ploughs, axes, scythes, and knives. The Acadians acquired their furs from the Indians for bread, peas, beans, prunes, tobacco, iron cooking pots, hatchets, iron arrow points, awls, casks, blankets and all manner of commodities.

In view of their brisk trading activities and the evidence of wealth found in Pictou County by the early English settlers, it appears that the tradition of caches buried by the expelled Acadians leaves treasure hunters with a load of dreams to follow.

It may be only a matter of time and diligent research before an Acadian cache of substantial value is uncovered.

NOTES

CHAPTER TWO
1. An inscribed stone found near Yarmouth, Nova Scotia, in 1812. The inscription on the stone is believed to have been carved by Leif Ericson in the year 1,007 and has been interpreted to read "Leif to Eric Raises (this monument)."
2. An implement thought to be a Norse axe although archaeologists contend it is of eighteenth- or nineteenth-century vintage.

CHAPTER SIX
1. A pod auger is designed to bring up cores of drilled material by the screwing motion of the chisel-tipped auger (a tool for boring holes in the earth with a sharp end for cutting, and spiral grooves for channelling the cuttings out of the hole).
2. A long podlike container equipped with a valve at the bottom to prevent the contents from dropping out.
3. About 12 ft. of the overburden soil has been removed during previous excavation work, so the drillers recorded depths less than originally existed. The approximate 160-ft. depth is also said to vary 10 ft. up or down in some places.
4. Carbon dating is a method of establishing the approximate age of carbonaceous remains, such as wood, by measuring the amount of radioactive carbon-14 left.

CHAPTER NINE
1. There is also an "Oak Island" off MacKenzie Point in Fox Harbour, Cumberland County, on the Northumberland Strait.

CHAPTER SIXTEEN
1. Louisbourg was captured by the British in 1745 after a forty-nine-day siege. It was later returned to France but again taken by the British in 1758. It is reasonable to presume that the siege referred to by the early settlers was that of 1745 as it is commonly known as "the siege of Louisbourg."

BIBLIOGRAPHY

Acadiensis Press. *They Planted Well: New England Planters in Maritime Canada*. Fredericton: Acadiensis Press, 1988.

Armstrong, Bruce. *Sable Island*. Toronto: Doubleday Canada Limited, 1981.

Baigent, Michael; Leigh, Richard and Lincoln, Henry. *The Holy Blood and the Holy Grail*. London: Transworld Publishers Ltd., 1990.

Bradley, Michael. *Holy Grail Across the Atlantic: The Secret History of Canadian Discovery and Exploration*. Willowdale, Ont.: Hounslow Press, 1988.

Calnek, W. A. *History of the County of Annapolis*. Toronto: William Briggs, 1897.

Campbell, Lyall. *Sable Island Shipwrecks: Disaster and Survival at the North Atlantic Graveyard*. Halifax: Nimbus Publishing Limited, 1994.

_____. *Sable Island, Fatal and Fertile Crescent*. Hantsport, N.S.: Lancelot Press, 1974.

Crooker, William S. *Oak Island Gold*. Halifax: Nimbus Publishing Limited, 1993.

_____. *The Oak Island Quest*. Windsor, N.S.: Lancelot Press, 1978.

Crowell, Bill. *Atlantic Treasure Troves*. Hantsport, N.S.: Lancelot Press, 1985.

Blomidon Naturalists Society. *A Natural History of Kings County, Nova Scotia*. Wolfville, N.S.: Acadia University, 1993.

Daniel, Glyn. *The Prehistoric Chamber Tombs of France: A Geographical, Morphological and Chronological Survey*. London: Thames and Hudson, 1960.

_____. *The Megalith Builders of Western Europe*. Baltimore: Penguin Books Inc., 1963.

Eaton, Arthur, W. H. *The History of Kings County*. Salem, Mass.: The Salem Press Company, 1910.

Fell, Barry. *America BC*. New York: Quadrangle/The New York Times Book Co., 1976.

Gray, Noreen and Annie A. Smith. *History Along the Old Guysborough Road*. Enfield, N.S.: Published by the authors, 1987.

Hichens, Walter W. *Island Trek*. Hantsport, N.S.: Lancelot Press, 1982.

Joussaume, Roger. *Dolmens for the Dead: Megalith-Building Throughout the World*. New York: Cornell University Press, 1988.

Keough, Pat And Rosemarie. *Wild and Beautiful Sable Island*. Fulford Harbour, B.C.: Nahanni Productions Inc., 1993.

Liverpool Symposium. *Megalithic Enquiries in the West of Britain*. Liverpool University Press, 1969.

Mclennan, J. S. *Louisbourg: From its Foundation to its Fall*. Halifax: The Book Room Limited, 1979.

Minister of Supply and Services Canada. *The Wreck of the* Auguste. National Historic Sites Parks Services: Environment Canada, 1992.

More, James F. *The History of Queens County, N. S.* Halifax: Nova Scotia Printing Company, 1873.

Nesmith, Robert I. *Dig for Pirate Treasure.* New York: The Devin-Adair Company, 1959.

Patterson, Rev. George. *A History of the County of Pictou, Nova Scotia.* Montreal: Dawson Brothers, 1877.

_____. *Sable Island: Its History and Phenomena.* Toronto: Trans. Roy. Soc. anada, Section II, 1894.

Pohl, Frederick J. *Atlantic Crossings Before Columbus.* New York:W. W. Norton nd Company, Inc., 1961.

Renfrew, Colin. *Before Civilization.* New York: Alfred A. Knopf, Inc., 1973.

Ross, Sally and Alphonse Deveau. *The Acadians of Nova Scotia Past and Present.* Halifax: Nimbus Publishing Limited, 1992.

Sherwood, Ronald H. *Legends, Oddities and Facts from the Maritime Provinces.* Hantsport, N.S.: Lancelot Press, 1984.

_____. *Pictou's Past.* Hantsport, N.S.: Lancelot Press, 1988.

_____. *Sagas of the Land and Sea.* Hantsport, N.S.: Lancelot Press, 1980.

Smith, I. F. *Windmill Hill and Avebury: Excavations by Alexander Keiller 1925-1939.* London: Oxford University Press, 1965.

Snow, Edward Rowe. *Ghosts, Gales and Gold.* New York: Dodd, Mead and Company, 1972.

_____. *Secrets of the North Atlantic Islands.* New York: Dodd, Mead and Company, 1950.

_____. *Strange Tales from Nova Scotia to Cape Hatteras.* New York: Dodd, Mead and Company, 1949.

_____. *True Tales of Buried Treasure.* (Revised edition). New York: Dodd, Mead and Company, 1962.

_____. *True Tales of Pirates and Their Gold.* New York: Dodd, Mead and Company, 1962.

_____. *Unsolved Mysteries of Sea and Shore.* New York: Dodd, Mead and Company, 1963.

Thom, A. *Megalithic Sites in Britain.* Oxford: Clarendon Press, 1967.

Zinck, Jack. *Shipwrecks of Nova Scotia, Volume 1.* Hantsport, N.S.:Lancelot Press, 1975.

_____. *Shipwrecks of Nova Scotia, Volume 2.* Hantsport, N.S.: Lancelot Press, 1977.